W9-CVS-208

ckout from v~

ꝫ.

ETHIOPIAN JEWS

THE STORY OF A MISSION

Frederick Musse

BY
ERIC PAYNE

Foreword
by
J. R. W. Stott

200 6609

© Eric Payne 1972
The Olive Press
16 Lincoln's Inn Fields, London, W.C.2.

BV
3560
.P33
c.2

CONTENTS

Chapter

FOREWORD

The idea that there may be African Jews comes as a surprise, even a shock, to many people. African Christians, African Muslims, African pagans they have heard of, but African Jews? It sounds almost a contradiction in terms. Well, of course, there are *white* African Jews, mining gold and diamonds in South Africa, living in affluence in Johannesburg and largely repudiating the faith of their fathers. But can there really be *black* African Jews, living in huts in the Ethiopian tableland, earning their livelihood by weaving and farming, and clinging tenaciously to the Old Testament?

It is about these Felasha Jews that Eric Payne writes in this book, drawing on his researches and his own experience of 22 years among them.

The origins of all the Ethiopian people are largely lost in the mists of antiquity. Eric Payne reminds us of God's word through Zephaniah in the 7th century BC that offerings would be brought to him 'from beyond the rivers of Ethiopia', and he suggests that the forbears of these Ethiopians may well have been Jewish traders from as far back as Solomon's day.

It seems certain, in any case, that Semitic immigrants not only intermarried with the Hamitic natives but also converted them to the Jewish faith, and that it is from this mixed race that both the Amharas (Ethiopia's leading tribe) and the Felashas are descended. What is particularly fascinating is that both peoples, though to a different degree, exhibit their Jewish ancestry.

The Amharas, both the Emperor and the people of Ethiopia, became Christian in the 4th century AD, and their first bishop was consecrated by the great Athanasius of Alexandria. This gave the Ethiopian church its links with the 'orthodox' tradition of Christendom. Its subsequent isolation—not least because of its mountainous inaccessibility—largely accounts both for its resistance to Islam which swept over North Africa in the 7th and 8th centuries and for the peculiar ethos which it has developed. For alongside its Christian traditions (some of which, like the veneration of the

5

Virgin Mary, are corrupt) it has preserved some ancient Jewish symbolism and ceremony. Its churches are built in compartments like the Jerusalem temple and cherish a model of the ark of the covenant. And many of its customs regarding birth and death, circumcision and diet, sabbath observance, liturgical music, feasts and fasts are derived from the Old Testament.

If the Amharas have retained in their Church these traces of Judaism, the Felasha Jews have somehow managed to preserve intact, and bring even into the latter part of the twentieth century, all the ancient practices of the Old Testament. In addition to such rites as circumcision and sabbath observance, which they share with the Amhara Christians, they still offer all the animal sacrifices prescribed in Leviticus (and are the only Jews in the world to do so), and they still observe the three annual Jewish festivals and the Day of Atonement.

This dual religious background of Ethiopia—the unreformed Ethiopian Orthodox Church of the Amharas and the equally unreformed Judaism of the Felashas—has presented Protestant missions with a formidable and complex problem.

Eric Payne describes what he calls 'the two plans' to Christianize Ethiopia, which were both initiated in the middle of the last century. He traces the 'spiritual' plan to Samuel Gobat who in 1846 became Anglican Bishop in Jerusalem, and the 'political' plan to the colourful Emperor Theodore, crowned in 1855, whose grandiose ambitions were first to unite his country by spreading Christianity and then to conquer the world by capturing Jerusalem! The interaction of these two processes makes an absorbing study.

Two particular characteristics of the Christian missionary enterprise in Ethiopia caught my attention and won my admiration as I read Eric Payne's book in manuscript.

The first I will call the *resolve to identify,* that is, the determination of these missionaries to become one with the Amharas and the Felashas, in so far as they were able.

Not that this ideal was entirely clear from the first or that it has always been fulfilled. For example, some of the nineteenth century missionaries (German and Swiss as well as British) were understandably the children of their times and shared some of the 'imperialistic' and 'paternalistic' attitudes of their day. There was a tendency among them to avoid over-familiarity with the 'natives' as something slightly unbecoming in European gentlefolk. And those were the days when British missionaries were also very conscious of being British subjects who, when under duress, could send a personal appeal to Queen Victoria and confidently expect an immediate dispatch of Her Majesty's troops to come to their rescue.

Against this contemporary background, the missionary policy adopted from the start was the more remarkable. The earliest missionaries sent in by Bishop Gobat were artisans—a gunsmith, a builder and an engraver—who were to earn their living by their trade, teach it to the Ethiopians and, so far as it was permitted, preach the gospel and distribute Bibles.

Permission to do this missionary work was granted by the Orthodox Bishop of all Ethiopia, on condition that any converts from among the Felashas would be baptized into the Ethiopian Orthodox Church. The first converts were so baptized in 1862, sixty-five of them in one year.

The acceptance of this policy by the missionaries implied their willingness to work within the Ethiopian Church (and to work for reform and renewal within it), and their undertaking not to found a separate and rival church of their own. It is not surprising that this policy decision aroused controversy—especially in more recent years among Lutheran missionaries—but it appears under God to have been the right decision. C.M.J. now have increasing opportunities within the Church itself. Roger Cowley is engaged in writing and translation work, his book on the Creeds having recently been published by the Orthodox Cathedral in Addis Ababa. He is also teaching Bible in the Bishop's School in Makalle, as well as Hebrew and Bible to priests. An increasing number of these appear to be hungry for the Word of God.

Eric Payne himself first reached Addis in 1946 as an army chaplain. Two years later, now demobilized and a missionary, he established the centre near Dabat. This has grown to a village of about 40 huts, with its own kitchen garden, orchard, well and livestock to make it a selfsupporting community. The buildings, he writes, were deliberately 'simple country style, with food, clothes and all amenities to match'.

What (out of modesty) he omits to tell us is that, in order to identify with those he was seeking to serve, he felt it right to observe all the feasts and fasts of the Ethiopian Orthodox Church, and that this probably undermined his health.

He also pioneered the concept of a residential Families' Bible School. This has enabled husbands and wives to learn together, and whole families to be exposed over a long period of 2 or 3 years to the influence of Christian teaching, example and fellowship. Then these established and trained Christian families have been able to go back to their own villages as ambassadors of Christ, earning their own living as before and not becoming paid agents of a foreign mission. This practical outworking of indigenous principles is most impressive.

The second characteristic of Christian missionaries in Ethiopia which is likely to strike every reader, as it struck me, is their *resolve to endure*. The record of one and a half centuries of missionary labour there has been one of hardship and danger borne with great fortitude.

For from its beginning the work of Protestant missionaries in Ethiopia has been beset with every conceivable difficulty. Eric Payne tells horrific tales of the sufferings of some early missionaries who were put in prison and in chains, robbed and beaten. The early converts suffered for their faith as well, like the 30 Felasha families who were brutally murdered by fanatical Muslim dervishes because they refused to acknowledge Mahomet and deny Christ.

In addition, there have been setbacks occasioned by famine and plague; by civil strife and war, in particular the Italian occupation of the country from 1935 to 1941, which included Mussolini's expulsion of all non-Catholic missionaries; by opposition and competition from other groups, from Muslims, from the Jewish counter-mission (at one time supported by the Israeli government), and from cults like Jehovah's Witnesses; by restrictive legislation and troublesome litigation; by tension among missionaries on questions of doctrine and policy; and by ill-health. Eric Payne passes lightly over his own domestic problems, over his wife's ill-health which led to their return to England, and over the tragic accident to their baby Elizabeth which has left her permanently handicapped.

It takes great courage to persevere in the face of odds like these. Missionaries seem to be a special target for diabolical attack. One cannot help admiring the Christian valour with which they endure their trials and refuse to become dispirited.

* * *

I am glad to commend this book to the Christian public, and hope that many will read and ponder its story. We at All Souls are proud to have three of our church members serving with C.M.J. in Ethiopia—Roger and Jean Cowley at Makalle engaged in educational work and Sally Teal, a nurse, who works in the clinic at Mach'a. May God use Eric Payne's valuable little book to stimulate many to pray for the growth and the reform of the Ethiopian Church, and perhaps to call some to go and serve it.

All Souls Church,   John Stott
Langham Place,   Christmas 1971
London W.1.

PREFACE

I would like to thank those friends who encouraged me to write this book, especially when it needed to be shortened, and most of all the former General Secretary of C.M.J., the Reverend Canon W. A. Curtis, and the lady who so kindly typed two different manuscripts, Miss L. M. Walker.

———————

Quotations from the Bible are from the Revised Standard Version unless otherwise stated, Copyright 1946 and 1952, and used by permission.

NOTE ON TRANSLITERATION OF ETHIOPIAN WORDS

Ethiopian names of places and people have been transliterated into English, bearing in mind the way they are pronounced in Amharic, and the way an Englishman would be likely to write down those sounds. For this reason the frequently used French "é" has been discarded in favour of the more English "ey".

Consonants followed by an apostrophe are explosives, pronounced with emphasis, and separated from the following vowel by a slight explosion of breath. Instances of this are the battle of Mek'dela which is usually written as Magdala in English books, and the lake T'ana.

When an Ethiopian name has an English equivalent which is considerably different, and yet better known to Englishmen, the English equivalent has been used. So for instance King Teywodros is called King Theodore, and King Yohannis is called King John. And the commonest spelling is kept for the Emperor Haile Selassie.

1
ETHIOPIA

The Country

ETHIOPIA is a vast land stretching to the south of the "Red
Sea", which was so called because of a legend that the blood
of gods was spilt there. It has for long been a land of mystery
to the rest of the world because it was protected by hot,
inhospitable deserts and steep escarpments. The population
lives on the high tableland, which is split up by huge river
gorges. These gorges are so steep that there is not a single
navigable river in the country, but the resulting mountain
scenery is all the more majestic.

Modern Ethiopia is more than four times the size of Great
Britain, yet it has only about a third of its population. Much
of the lowland especially is empty by European standards. Of
the 13 provinces, Tigrey, Begemdir, Gojam, Wello, and
Shewa, with Eritrea are the real core of Ethiopia, the remaining provinces having been incorporated only fairly recently.
Each of these six provinces is about as large as England, and
together they include most of the high tableland, 5,000-10,000
feet above sea level. Ethiopia has only two seasons, a rainy
season from mid June to mid September, and a dry season.

The people

Its 23 million or so people are as varied and changeable
as the land they occupy, and they speak about 70 different
languages. Long before Christ, Hamitic peoples occupied these
tablelands and drove the Nilotic tribes down to the hot lowlands. Later Semitic tribes crossed from South Arabia. They
brought with them the use of metals, and higher forms of
agriculture and irrigation, and above all a new culture.

These Semites were always a minority and they intermarried with the Hamites until they were no longer distin-
guishable, but their culture was dominant. The Semitised
Hamites became the ruling tribe of today, the Amharas.
They are a handsome race, a little bigger than the Arabs of

South Arabia, a slightly darker brown and with more black curly hair, but easily distinguistable from the negroes of the lowlands.

Ethiopians have a respect for the farmer and the priest but not for craftsmen nor for traders. Most of all they admire the warrior, and their highest titles are military in origin.

The Ethiopian villages of 10 to 20 round thatched huts are sited on defensible hill tops, or on well-drained slopes, rather than in the valleys. If we follow a peasant and his wife into their hut, we notice that they have but few wants and dress very simply. Men wear tight-fitting trousers and a shirt both of white cotton, with a sort of Roman toga on top of all. Women wear a voluminous skirt of rougher homespun material. Few country people have much furniture or even stores. They see little point in building up large stores for the future, for in the past these only attracted the attention of stronger chiefs with more warriors, and now they attract taxes and thieves. Their only furniture is basket tables which can easily be moved, and bins for the corn made of sun-baked mud and straw. There are no shops in the country areas, so even today each household does most things for itself: grinding the corn, baking the bread, drawing the water, making the beer and slaughtering for meat. We notice the chickens in the house and the place for the donkeys or mule! Outside the hut the only fence is not around any field but to enclose two small areas, one for the cattle, and one for the sheep or goats.

As this story starts more than a century ago we will try to picture the people of those days and note their characteristics.

Mountain dwellers as isolated as these were bound to become over-confident, proud and ignorant. They were sure that no foreign land was as good as theirs or grew as fine corn. No foreign soldiers could stand up to theirs, nor was there any church so holy and orthodox. Christianity for most was not a matter of creed, but a national caste system whose ceremonies gave them a sense of superiority over others.

Great contrasts in the scenery helped to bring about great contrasts in their character. They were brave individualists yet 'fear of men', fear of what a neighbour may say or do to them, was very characteristic. They showed little sense of shame for any crimes, but could never stand being insulted. They could be cruel to enemies, yet their magnanimity recently for instance towards the Italians and the Ethiopians who served them was quite remarkable. They have always regarded themselves as superior to all foreigners and so were suspicious of them, yet they were usually most courteous and friendly towards individual foreigners. They were a very religious people, but lacked depth of spiritual understanding. It is these opposites in their character which account for the many different estimates of these people and which puts such a question mark over their future.

Their History

The history of Ethiopia is chiefly the history of its Church. Apart from the seventeenth-century castles at Gonder, almost everything ancient is of a religious nature. Even the steles found at Axum bore images of the palaces in the world to come reserved for the souls of pagan kings, whose bodies were usually buried beneath them. These huge carved blocks of stone are taller than the obelisks of Egypt, and end in a curved image of the vault of heaven rather than in a point. They illustrate the formidable power and engineering abilities of the Kings of Axum not long after the time of Christ.

The history of the Church does not start with the Ethiopian eunuch of the eighth chapter of Acts, for he was of the ancient Biblical Ethiopia or Nubia, and of the Kingdom of Meroe which is now Moslem and part of the Sudan.

Its history starts with Frumentius, who was one of two Syrian lads wrecked on the coast of Eritrea in the early part of the fourth century. The local people found them praying under a tree and took them to their king at Axum. Frumentius became his secretary, the tutor to his son, and eventually the virtual regent of the country when the king died. When the son came of age Frumentius was permitted to go back to his home country, but he only got as far as Egypt, where he besought the Bishop of Alexandria, the famous Athanasius, to send a bishop and some priests to Axum, which he believed was ripe for conversion to Christianity. Athanasius consecrated Frumentius himself as bishop and sent Him back.

Through him the Emperor and eventually much of Ethiopia became Christian.

In the fifth century the Egyptian Church, together with her daughter Church in Axum, split from the main body of Christendom. By this time the kings of Axum were at the height of their power. Less than a century later one of them sent a large army across the Red Sea and conquered a king in Southern Arabia who had become Jewish in faith and was vigorously persecuting Christians. Memories of this gave substance to the later medieval legend of Prester John, the mysterious Christian Priest-King who ruled somewhere beyond the Moslem occupied countries.

During the next century Mohammed was born, and the forces of Islam conquered Egypt, North Africa and most of the Persian Empire. To make sure of the loyalty of the daughter Church, the Monophysite Patriarch in Egypt forged a Canon of the Council of Nicaea (which had been held before the Ethiopian Church even existed) to the effect that the Ethiopian Church should always come under the jurisdiction of the Coptic Patriarch in Egypt.

The Moslems in South Arabia did not attack their neighbours across the Red Sea for a long time, partly because the kings of Axum had harboured some relatives of Mohammed when he was being persecuted in Arabia. When they eventually occuped the few ports on the south side of the Red Sea, they cut off the Axumites from the rest of the Christian world. At the same time a Hamitic tribe overran and occupied most of their territory in Eritrea and forced the Axumites to migrate more to the south, to the Province of Begemdir.

Here they came up against several Agau tribes, only one of which, the Felasha Jews, had been semitised as much as themselves. These resisted the gospel strongly, but many of the pagan Agaus became Christian, and then those of Lasta actually ruled Ethiopia for a long time, claiming to be descendants of Moses and his Ethiopian wife.[a] During this time the religious and intellectual life of Ethiopia suffered a decline.

The Axumite kings had been strengthened in their authority

(a) Numbers 12, 1 (A.V.)

by a legend to the effect that the Queen of Sheba, when she visited King Solomon, had had a son by him who became King of Ethiopia as Menelik the First, and who managed to substitute a copy of the Ark of the Covenant in Jerusalem, given to him by Solomon, and bring the real one to Axum. The priests taught that in Solomon was planted a pearl, which was passed on from father to son and eventually became the Virgin Mary, from whom Christ was born. This legend became extremely important for the unity of Ethiopia, for through it the people came to believe that they were the chosen of God in the place of the Jews who had rejected the Messiah, custodians of the Ark in their place, and ruled over by kings descended from Solomon, and, through that pearl, related to Christ Himself.

When a Shewan prince seized power from the Agau dynasty of Lasta in the thirteenth century partly through the leader of the Church, he claimed to be of the original Solomonic line, with the result that the Church supported him all the more, and was rewarded with such wealth and favour that it rapidly deteriorated still further spiritually.

Belief in this legend, helped the people to survive the constant wars with Moslem tribes to the north-east, and eventually the virtual conquest and occupation of their land for ten years in the sixteenth century under Ahmed the left handed.

After this, Portuguese Jesuits entered Ethiopia and succeeded in persuading one or two of the later kings to profess Roman Catholicism. When these tried to force the whole nation to follow them there were civil wars, and in the end Orthodoxy triumphed and the Jesuits were turned out. The eighteenth century and the first half of the nineteenth was a period like that of the judges in Israel when "every man did what was right in his own eyes".

The Ethiopian Church

The Orthodox Church of Ethiopia has been isolated from all others for so long that it is unique.

Many of the customs of the early church which it received in the fourth century it has preserved faithfully to this day. Before the days of Constantine, as Christians had to work on Sundays, they held their services before dawn; the Ethiopians have kept to this time for most of their services. Also in the early church the members of the congregation gave one another a kiss of peace at the end of their services.[b] Later a holy book, or else just a piece of wood called the "pax board," was passed around for each to kiss. At the end of the service in an Ethiopian Church the members of the congregation nearest to the sanctuary are usually invited to kiss either the service book, or the hand of the priest who consecrated the elements, or the cross he always carries with him. The emphasis upon Easter and lack of emphasis upon Christmas are also typical of the early church. Unfortunately some of its customs and teachings have been corrupted over the years. The emphasis upon the saints and martyrs, and above all the veneration of the Virgin Mary, is carried to an extreme. In spite of this there are many good living men, and the average Ethiopian has absorbed sufficient true Christianity to make his laws, religion and social customs superior to those of most other African nations and to keep him from the worst cruelties.

The priests are usually married. They live from their fields like most of the rest of the population and from the dues given at baptisms, burials and memorial feasts. They know most of the different forms of the church service by heart, but little of its meaning. Still less, therefore, are they expected to know the Bible or the doctrines of their Church, and up to now the ignorance of most of those in the country parts has been shocking. It is therefore impossible for them to be anything other than conservative.

Their influence is very great, for every family must have its own father confessor; excommunication by him is greatly feared.

In the services they are helped by debteras (learned men), who are trained in all kinds of hymn singing and books in Giiz, the dead ecclesiastical language. They are also helped by deacons, who are always young boys. These are ordained in large groups by the Abuna or bishop, by his breathing upon them. They stop serving at puberty.

(b) 1 Cor. 16.20

Most high offices are held by monks. Until recently there was never more than one bishop for the whole of Ethiopia, and he had to be a monk, an Egyptian Copt consecrated by the Patriarch in Egypt and rarely knowing Amharic or Giiz. But now the Church in Ethiopia is independent, and should not be called Coptic but Ethiopian Orthodox.

Old Testament Ways

Very many Old Testament customs have survived among the Amhara Christians from before the fourth century when most of them were of the Jewish religion.

An Ethiopian Church is counted as consecrated only when it has in it the "tabot", which is erroneously described in most books about Ethiopia as a model of the Ark of the Covenant of the Old Testament.[c] There is such a model, but it is a sort of cupboard with an open cupola at the top, on which the "tabot" rests. The "tabot" is a flat block of wood, which is blessed by the Bishop and carried on the heads of the priests in important processions wrapped up in coloured cloths. So it is a sort of portable altar, which might be described as a model of the tables of the Law which Moses placed inside the Ark,[d] and like them it usually has written on it the Ten Commandments. Many Ethiopians still believe that the Church at Axum contains the real Ark of the Covenant.

Like the Temple, the Churches in Ethiopia theoretically have three sections.[e] Only the two priests and the three deacons who are consecrating the elements on the "tabot", are allowed in the innermost Holy of Holies, or Sanctuary, which, like that of the Temple, is at the very least veiled off from public view.

When you see the choirmen singing the liturgies, which have been influenced by those of the Temple and the synagogue, watch them accompanying them with a leaning stick in one hand and a sistrum in the other, and hear the rhythm of the drum, you will forget that you are in a Christian Church and think you are back in the days of the Old Testament.[f] When the women occasionally join in with their high-pitched "illillill" (something like the Hebrew 'Allelujahs') the metamorphosis

(c) Deut 31.26   (d) Deut. 10.5   (e) Heb. 9.6 & 7.   (f) 2 Sam 6.14.

will be complete, especially if it is at night with waxed tapers as the only light.

From birth to death the life of an Ethiopian Christian is guided by Old Testament customs. Baby boys are circumcised on the eighth day as with the Jews,[g] not at five or six years old, as with the Copts of Egypt; though this is no longer a religious rite and never done in the Church. In fact, both mother and child are regarded as unclean until the fortieth day with a boy, or the eightieth with a girl,[h] when the mother is cleansed with holy water and the child baptised.

In his daily life also the Ethiopian is constantly portraying the Old Testament, with his "salutations in the market places" when the name of God is frequently heard.[i] If he wishes to eat meat he will almost certainly slaughter it himself, making sure that all the blood is drained away.[j] Never would he eat what a man of a different faith has slaughtered, nor any meat which the Old Testament calls unclean.[k] The Amharas have not derived this from the Copts of Egypt, who eat pork for instance, which suggests that such prejudices must be of Jewish origin and earlier than the fourth century. Like the Jews of old an Amhara prefers never to eat anything with any man who is not a Christian[l] and like them again he will fast twice a week.[m] He will also keep various monthly feasts according to his own calendar, which is based on the ancient Egyptian one, and starts with New Year's Day in September (as with the Jews) and with New Year thoughts and customs which are Jewish in origin.

If he is a farmer, as most Ethiopians are, he will observe Saturday as his Sabbath as well as Sunday by abstaining from all ploughing, weeding or reaping. If he has killed a man by accident he may well try to escape the resulting blood feud by fleeing to a "city of Refuge", that is to a church administered area, to obtain the protection of the priests.[n] And when he dies the funeral procession will make seven stops to the grave, and he will be specially remembered on the third, tenth and fortieth day after, as with some Jews.

(g) Gen. 17.12.   (h) Lev 12.3-5.
(i) Ruth 2.4; Lk 20.46.   (j) Lev. 3.17.   (k) Lev. 11. 3-8.
(l) Acts 11.3.   (m) Luke 18.12.
(n) Num. 35.11.

2
THE FELASHA JEWS

THE NAME 'Felasha' means 'immigrant' and is that applied
to them by others, but hardly ever by themselves. They call
themselves 'Beyta Israel', 'the House of Israel'. The names
alone suggest that many of their ancestors were immigrants
from Israel.

The Felashas themselves do not know when these ancestors
came. Most of them repeat the legend of Menelik, because
they are scattered amongst the Amharas, and they will tell
you that they are descended from the sons of Jewish nobles
whom Solomon compelled to go to Ethiopia with his son
Menelik. Jeremiah's contemporary, Zephaniah, knew that
some Jews had reached Ethiopia already by then, for he says
"From beyond the rivers of Ethiopia my suppliants, the
daughter of my dispersed ones, shall bring my offering".° The
only Jews who have ever lived beyond the river Nile and its
large tributary, the Atbara, or the T'ekezey as it is called in
Ethiopia, are the Felasha Jews. Zephaniah lived more than
600 years before Christ. So it may be that their ancestors were
Jewish traders from as far back as the days of Solomon, who
intermarried with these Agau people and converted them to
the Jewish faith.

The main centre of the Felashas used to be in Simeyn, an
area just south of the T'ekezey, in the northern part of the
Province of Begemdir. Now they are scattered throughout that
province with a few in the adjacent ones.

There is a tradition (recorded in the book Kibre Negest)
that in the days before Ethiopia became Christian half of its
people were obedient to the Jewish faith and half worshipped
the serpent. Strangely enough, the former was stronger among
the Agaus and the poorer classes, whilst the upper classes of
the Axumites were heathen. With the Felashas the Jewish
customs became strong and exclusive; with the Amharas they
became inclusive, being assimilated into their Christian faith.

(o) Zeph. 3.10.

The Felashas are therefore no more Semitic (and no less) than the Amharas. That is why it is impossible to tell which is which by their looks, though one can occasionally tell a Felasha woman by the kind of necklace she wears and by her short cropped hair. Ethnically the evidence for their Jewish descent is very slight, but religiously they are Jews, although not rabbinically acceptable. To deny this would be to deny the fact that a man of any race may become a Jew by accepting that faith plus circumcision and other initiatory rites.[p]

Their History

The first traveller to mention the Felashas was Eldad the Danite in the ninth century. He believed that they were part of the lost ten tribes of Israel. Up to three centuries before him the Jews had become so strong in South Arabia that they ruled over a large part of it, but had been conquered and persecuted from the seventh century onwards, and some of these were probably the last immigrants to join the Felashas. In the tenth century they were so strong that they helped a heathen Agau queen to destroy the Axumite royal family and lived in reasonable security until the fourteenth century.

From then until the seventeenth century there were several wars, with the Amharas ultimately victorious. The Felashas were deprived of all land and forced to live in separate communities scattered throughout the Province of Begemdir. They became the artisans for the Amharas, the smiths, weavers, potters and builders, and for these purposes some were deported to other parts of Ethiopia, where they usually became nominal Christians known as 'Tebiban'.

In the nineteenth century a large number of Felashas, urged on by a Felasha monk, who claimed to have seen a vision, tried to go to Jerusalem. They crossed the T'ekezey river into Tigrey, and circled the Christian Cathedral city of Axum seven times. Joshua had done this to Jericho at the orders of God and so conquered it,[q] and by doing this they believed they would force the Christian priests of Axum to return to them the Ark of the Covenant to take back to Jerusalem. To their dismay they received nothing but blows and insults. Many

(p) Ex. 12.48,49; Esth. 8.17.　　　　(q) Josh. 6.4, 15 & 20.

died of hunger and malaria, and while most of the remainder settled in the southern part of Tigrey north of the river T'ekezey, some went to the area of its source in Lasta.

Their Leaders

During the fifteenth century, a Christian monk named Abba Sivra, who was attracted to the Old Testament prophets, strongly condemned the corruption and unbiblical ways at the court of the King, just as the prophets had done. He was persecuted by the Christians but eventually welcomed by the Felashas, among whom he lived the life of a hermit in a cave. Large numbers of Felashas who lived similarly in those troublous times looked to him as their revered leader. Their successors were reverenced to such an extent that when the last Felasha political leader, Gideon, was conquered, the Felashas turned to the Jewish monks for leadership. These monks were maintained by the tithes of the Felashas, and lived in compounds next to the synagogues, which were then made with two rooms, or three if there was also a community of nuns, so that no ordinary Felasha came into contact with these 'holy' men and women. The three rooms were not one within the other, nor inspired by the Temple pattern as with the Christians, but put up side by side with no doors between because of this desire for separation, which became the key-note of their religion. Even ordinary Felasha men and women bathed themselves and washed their clothes after going to the market or having any close contact with the Christians, who began to call them the "Don't touch me's".

For centuries these Felashas thought that they were the only Jews in the world. When they met European Jews they were surprised at the disapproval that most of them expressed about their 'unorthodox' practices, especially that of the monks in making eunuchs of themselves, which they showed to be unscriptural.'

Fewer and fewer young men came forward to be monks, and the last of these in a position of authority died at the age of about 100 in 1965. Two nuns and one monk only remain in Simeyn but these have no authority.

(r) Deut. 23.1

This does not mean the end of the Felasha faith, but it could mean simply a return to the days before Abba Sivra, with one roomed synagogues (which practically all of them are already), and other Chief Priests replacing the monks as the bishops, as it were. These Chief Priests are now chosen from among the others by their fellows without ceremony on the basis of their superior knowledge of Giiz and ability to translate the old Felasha language, because all now speak Amharic. The old Felasha language is a dialect of Agau and very similar to both Quarinnia and K'imantinnia. The Felashas know nothing of the Jewish religious books called the Talmud, so their religious leaders are not rabbis but these priests. The most distinctive part of their duties, which is now rapidly dying out, is the offering of animal sacrifices.

Animal Sacrifices

Felashas are the only Jews who now offer sacrifices. The chief priest offers these on a large stone, surrounded by four or twelve other stones, or sometimes on a heap of 12 stones, near the synagogue. Through them they hope to persuade God to do what otherwise He would not, especially to forgive their sins.

These sacrifices include all those mentioned in the Old Testament, except that they make no distinction between a sin-offering and a guilt offering.[s] They also tend to confuse these with the burnt offering. For if a man wishes to offer a sin-offering for some great sin such as apostasy, or to make his peace with God shortly before his death, he will bring two animals, one of which must be a goat. This will be taken out into the bush by the Chief Priest and burnt completely. The man will then count his sins as burnt up and may go home without seeing the actual sin-offering sacrificed on the altar. For if there is only one Chief Priest he will remain in the bush until night, when he bathes himself and washes his clothes before returning home.[t] The next day he alone will offer the sin-offering, burn the blood with some salt and other parts of the animal as commanded in the Bible, and eat the remainder with his family.[u]

(s) Lev. 6.25 & 7.1.   (t) Lev. 22.6, 7.   (u) Lev. 4.35 & 6.26.

The Biblical Peace Offering is called by the Felashas the Salvation Offering, or the Vow Offering, according to its purpose. This is the most popular one because it is eaten by all.[v]

Peace Offerings are killed at their religious New Year (in March) Passover, Pentecost, the commemoration of Abraham, the day of Atonement, the Feast of Booths,[w] and at a feast now said to be in commemoration of the separation of the Israelites from others in the days of Ezra and Nehemiah.[x] This comes in November and seems to have been started by the monks. Two other important days for Peace Offerings are the feasts of the 'Seventh Sabbath' in August and in January, but these are not based on the Bible. When any man offers to produce the Peace Offering on any of the above feasts he usually keeps it up for the rest of his life, and looks on this as one guarantee of his salvation. These offerings are however only counted as actual sacrifices if a part is burnt.

Sacrifices are dying out largely because many Felashas now realise that they were not authorised away from Jerusalem and it is the observance of the Saturday Sabbath that is the most important part of the Felasha religion today.

The Saturday Sabbath

Shortly after mid-day on Friday the Felasha men, and especially the women, will bathe themselves and wash their clothes in the nearby river. The women then make the beer and the special loaves of bread which are the cereal offerings for the Sabbath.[y] All food is cold, for all fires will have been put out by sunset on Friday, but it is more abundant than on any other day, especially meat. No work is done on that day and there is no travelling.[z] This and their desire for separation prevents Felashas becoming traders.

The Felashas have gone further than any others in personifying the Sabbath. In what appears to be about the only book of largely Felasha origin, "The Commandments of the Sabbath," it is pictured as a woman, who is crowned by angels in heaven each Sabbath, and who plays a major part in

(v) Lev. 17.11 & 19.   (w) Lev. 23.5, 16, 27 & 34.
(x) Neh. 8.13; 9.2 & 10.30.   (y) Lev. 2.4-7.   (z) Ex. 16.23, 29.

delivering souls from Hell, and is indeed the Chief Mediator for the Felashas.

This book has so many thoughts which are evidently Arabic in origin that it cannot be older than the fourteenth century, and it probably goes back to Abba Sivra. If it is true that Abba Sivra was a coptic Abuna, as many Felashas maintain, the connection is the more likely, as his native language would have been Arabic. In which case this personification may have been a designed parallel to the position occupied by the Virgin Mary with the Ethiopian Christians.

Their Religion

The religion of the Felashas is based on the Old Testament and the yearly and monthly feasts. They do not know Hebrew, or rabbinic traditions, except in so far as they have in recent years learnt them from foreign Jews.

The yearly feasts in order of importance, consist of the "Seventh Sabbath"; Passover, when they eat a special un-leavened bread for a week;[a] the day of Atonement when the priests accompany their prayers by drums and bells and dance more than on other days; and the Feast of Booths, when they do no work for a week as at Passover but do not live in booths;[b] and finally Pentecost or Harvest. Like the Christians they commemorate these feasts also monthly by special prayers[c] and abstinence from work, though many now no longer honour these monthly days.

They have never observed any post-captivity Jewish feasts or customs, such as the feasts of Purim[d] or Chanukah, nor have they ever used Phylacteries[e] or Praying Shawls. They do not know the ceremony of Bar Mitsvah, when a Jewish boy is made a "Son of the Law", but have something like it. At fourteen years old (not thirteen) a boy will give money to a priest to become his "soul father", and in the past he used to have to bring a sin (and burnt) offering before he was counted as a full man. But there is no need for ten men in order to form a synagogue, as with the Jews elsewhere in

(a) Ex. **12.15.**
(b) Lev. 23.39-43.   (c) c.f. Num. 28.11   (d) Esth 9.26-28.
(e) Matt. 23.5.

the world, any priest can build his own house of prayer and collect a congregation regardless of numbers.

They do not place the same stress on fasting as the Christians, nor does their fasting consist of abstaining from all things coming from an animal. On a fast day the Felasha will eat nothing, and often drink nothing also, until after dark, when he may eat whatever he pleases and as much as he wants.

At the end of some of them, particularly the Day of Atonement, all take a little corn, usually to a hill top. There they pray for departed relatives by putting a pinch of corn on to a stone in the name of each one, and then leave it for the birds to eat.

The Felashas have no special confession or creed, but some believe, as the Christians used to do, that an Ethiopian Messiah will arise, named Theodore, who will deliver them and eventually all the world from evil. They got this from a Christian book entitled "Fikkarey Iyesus", "The Explanation of Jesus", which they copied and altered where necessary, calling it of course "Fikkarey Iyasu", "The Explanation of Joshua".

Daily Life

Their houses, dress, food and daily life generally are very like those of the Amharas among whom they are now scattered, though they have never eaten raw meat. But, as so many of them are artisans, doing work despised by the Amharas, they usually live on the outskirts of Amhara villages in groups of about three or four huts, for you cannot have too many weavers, let us say, in one area. Weavers are always men, and either Moslems or Felashas in Northern Ethiopia. The loom, which must be about the simplest kind in the world, is often made by the owner himself out of wood and set up under the eave of his hut. He sits with his legs from the knees in a pit dug in the earth, throwing his shuttle back and forth over the fabric. The buyer must supply the thread, made from raw cotton by the women of each household. So all clothing in the country is white, though many buy coloured cottons to be woven into the border, and the women like their dresses to be embroidered, usually with crosses. Embroidery too is a man's work, rarely a woman's. Nowadays even the Felasha women like to have their embroidered work in the form of a cross.

The weaver's neighbour may be a blacksmith. The smiths used to mine their iron from places where they found iron-stone on the surface, but since the Italian occupation they rely on scrap iron. The charcoal fire is made in a small hollow in the ground and the two simple bellows of sheep or goats' skins are worked rhythmically by one man, whilst a second takes out the red hot plough share and pounds it alternately with a third man on the anvil with an iron mallet. Payment is usually in grain rather than in money.

Most artisans are usually farmers also, but the land belongs to the Amharas, and the Felashas must pay rent for it at the rate of a quarter of the produce. Many Felashas are too poor to own two bulls and a plough as well as a loom. In such cases their wives usually help out by making simple pottery, shaped by hand without a wheel and fired without glazing. Such pots outside a hut, and the smoke rising from little mounds where others are being fired, and the shuttle or the noise of the smith's mallet, are the main ways of telling a Felasha village.

Outside most huts is a much smaller one, which is not to be found amongst the Amharas. This little hut is for the ceremonially unclean women, which means every mother for the first forty days after birth if the babe is a boy, and eighty days if a girl, and every woman for seven days of each month.[f] During this time relatives will give her bread or parched corn, and pour into her cup some drink without touching her, and meanwhile cook for the husband and family. If the community is very poor several families will share this hut, but if one family is particularly rich they may build another hut for the mother to occupy after the first eight days besides the little one referred to above. Men never use this hut. If they have become ceremonially unclean from carrying a corpse, for instance, they must live outside the village under a tree for a week and then bathe themselves before coming back. Fortunately for the Felashas, Ethiopia is a reasonably warm

(f) Lev. 12 3-5 & 15.19.

country! If a corpse is taken out of the main hut immediately after death that hut is not regarded as having become unclean.[g]

On the fortieth or eightieth day, when Amhara children are baptised, Felasha children also are sprinkled by the priest with holy water which used to be made holy with the ashes of a sacrificial red heifer as the Bible Commands,[h] and the priest will read over them the magic book of 'Disciples'. The children are regarded as safe from demons before then because they have not yet been named. The reading of this book is thought to protect them, particularly when all the magical names of God by which Moses was thought to have triumphed over Pharaoh are recited over the child.

The Felashas practice magic more than any other tribe of that area, claiming to control evil spirits, to foretell the future from the stars, and to protect from diseases or cure them, especially by amulets. They know that the Bible forbids witchcraft, but say that it is allowed when practised on Gentiles and not on Jews. In spite of this, and largely because of their separation from the others, they are the cleanest and most moral of those tribes.

When a girl is first married she is examined by elderly women before the end of the festivities. If she is found not to be a virgin she is excommunicated from the Felasha community, and the young man divorces her automatically with impunity even though he be a priest.* For divorce is regarded as a sin for priests, but not for ordinary Felashas. This would cause no heart-break to the man, because as in most Eastern countries, he may never have seen the girl before the festivities started, for his parents will have chosen her.

The Felashas have been declining in number for the last two centuries. There has never been a census taken of them. After questioning many from various areas over a period of twenty years I estimate that they now number about 25,000.

(g) Num. 19 14-19.   (h) Num. 19.2, 9, 11, 12.
* Is not this the explanation of our Lord's one exception as regards divorce for fornication, not adultery? For the Jews required a divorce to break a contract between engaged couples. Matt. 5.32 R.V.

3

TWO PLANS PUT INTO OPERATION

A Spiritual Plan

CONCERTED EFFORTS for missionary work were not made in England until the late eighteenth century, and even then the Church as a whole took so little interest that individuals had to band themselves together to form missionary societies. One of the first of these was the Church Missionary Society, formed in 1799, followed ten years later by what is now the Church's Ministry among the Jews. C.M.S. saw the possibilities that abounded if the ancient churches of the Armenians, Nestorians, Copts and Ethiopians could be revived and inspired to take the Gospel to the Moslems among whom they lived. The Basle Mission in Switzerland and Germany had had men with the same vision and readily made an alliance with C.M.S. C.M.J. had a similar vision with regard to the Jews once converted to Christ.

Samuel Gobat

Samuel Gobat, a French speaking Swiss, was trained at Basle. He then went to Paris for four years where his meeting many Jews led him to study Hebrew as well as Arabic. After this C.M.S. asked him to go to Ethiopia, and in 1826 he set out with a Swiss companion. They were delayed in Egypt for three years because Europeans were prohibited from entering Ethiopia, but, with the aid of a young Ethiopian monk, were able to learn Amharic there and also to obtain a stock of a book which consisted of the Gospels, Acts and Romans translated into Amharic by another Ethiopian monk. By 1829 they had become friends with the ambassador of the ruler of Tigrey. They travelled with him to Tigrey and later went on to Gonder, which was under a separate ruler.

At Gonder Gobat quickly won the friendship of many priests, and especially the Itchegey, Senior Monk of Ethiopia, by his gift of these books in Amharic. Every day he had many visitors, providing him with ample opportunities for witnessing to the Gospel, and a real interest was shown by both Amharas and Felashas. An outbreak of fighting between the two rulers had blocked the passes to Tigrey, and Gobat had brought only three months' supply of money for himself and the twelve men who carried his stock of books. He had been praying very much to know what to do, and after he had sent his last dollar to the market he suddenly remembered his gun. He took his baggage carriers out hunting, at which they became so adept that they never lacked for food, especially once he learned how to make gunpowder. When the fighting ended six months later he returned to Tigrey.

In 1833 Gobat went to Europe, and returned to Ethiopia two years later, this time with a wife, and accompanied by a gifted linguist, Dr. Isenberg. For the first time they were able to bring many copies of the whole Bible in Amharic. Unfortunately, Gobat and his wife became so ill during their stay at Adewa that they had to leave in 1836. C.M.S. replaced him the following year by Dr. Krapf, another man trained at St. Chrischona, but Dejjazmach Wubey, the ruler of Simeyn had, in the meantime, conquered the ruler of Tigrey and become very friendly with the Jesuits who had gained entrance to the land. In 1838 they persuaded him to banish the C.M.S. missionaries from his country. Isenberg and Krapf went to the ruler of Shewa, where Krapf found a life interest in the Galla people, while Isenberg returned to England in 1840 and composed the first Amharic dictionary and grammar in English.

About this time a new Abuna, or Bishop of all Ethiopia, had been consecrated in Egypt and sent to Ethiopia. He was a young man of 22 who had been educated in Cairo, partly by a C.M.S. missionary. It seemed as if the foundation was being laid for the revival of the Church in Ethiopia, but C.M.S. was then fully committed in other parts of the world and was unable to restart work in Ethiopia. But Gobat could never forget the spiritual needs of that country. He had been sent to Malta in 1839 to take charge of the C.M.S. Centre for translating and publishing literature in Arabic, and in 1846 was invited to become the second Anglican Bishop in Jerusalem. After his consecration Gobat quickly made plans to establish twelve new stations stretching from Jerusalem

through Egypt and the Sudan to the highlands of Ethiopia.
At the end of 1854 Bishop Gobat received six young men
trained at a new Bible School at St. Chrischona near Basle, and
decided the time was ripe to make a new beginning in
Ethiopia.

The Rise of Theodore with a political plan

Kasa, later Theodore, was the son of the ruler of Quara, a
small district near the Sudan border; his mother came from
Dembia, a sub province north of Lake T'ana. After she was
divorced they went through a time of great poverty and little
Kasa was sent to school at Chenker just east of Jenda. When
the place was sacked by the Galla ruler of Gonder, Kasa was
one of the few to escape, and fled to his older half brother,
Kinfu, the ruler of Dembia. Kinfu sent Kasa to school at a
monastery in Quara for nine years and it was here that he
learnt about "Fikkarey Iyesus", an apocryphal book written
in Giiz, the ancient Ethiopian language, which prophesied the
coming of a Saviour named Theodore to rule over Ethiopia.
Then followed three years in the army when Kinfu was
killed and Kasa had to flee. He became a powerful outlaw and
eventually Ras Ali, the Governor of Gonder, enlisted his
services and gave him his daughter in marriage.

Kasa's power grew rapidly, and by 1852 Ras Ali was so
alarmed by this that he gave Kasa's territories to the ruler of
Gojam. Kasa killed this ruler and went on to defeat Ras Ali
himself in 1853. The Abuna then agreed to reside in Gonder
if he banished the Jesuits from his territories.

Kasa's power still grew and in 1854 he attacked and
defeated the ruler of Simeyn, Dejjazmach Wubey. Two days
later, in February 1855, Kasa was crowned King of Kings of
Ethiopia by the Abuna in the Church of the capital of Simeyn.
To everyone's surprise the new Emperor took the throne name
of Theodore II.

Technically, Kasa did not now claim to be Emperor, but he
was making it clear that his claim was far more than to be
the chief Ras or Prince of Ethiopia, and far more than the
puppet emperor whom everyone ignored in Gonder. He
intended to fulfil the prophecies of the fifteenth century
apocryphal book Fikkarey Iyesus. The prophecy was that

after widespread fighting and famine Jesus Christ would bring to power a man named Theodore who, in the latter days, would rule for forty years. Poverty and war would be overcome and men would turn to the Lord, obeying Theodore and the Abuna. When the cities and churches of a united Ethiopia had been rebuilt, the righteousness, peace and prosperity of that blessed rule would be extended to all the world. Kasa's rise from poverty and above all his military successes, caused his followers to believe that he really was this Theodore, the Elect of God.

Theodore had plenty of courage allied to a humble manner, preferring to call himself "the slave of Christ", though by this he meant that human help or opposition were not of first importance. He announced his aims as: to unite and reform Ethiopia, to make the Christian faith dominant throughout the land, and then to become master of the world by capturing Jerusalem.

Charles Plowden was the first British Consul in Ethiopia and his reports to Britain were full of praise for Theodore and high hopes for the future. The disunity and fighting which had previously so hindered Gobat's work seemed to be ending and this led C.M.S. to ask Dr. Krapf to see what had happened to their property. He carried a letter from Bishop Gobat to the Emperor asking him for permission to send missionaries who would also teach his people trades. Dr. Krapf took as his companion one of the six men trained at St. Chrischona.

Martin Flad

Martin Flad was of good German peasant stock and felt the call to the mission field when he was ten years old. After his training at St. Chrischona, an elderly couple offered him all their property if he would stay and work in Europe, but he accepted the call to Ethiopia and after a year's study of Amharic under Isenberg he left to join Bishop Gobat in Jerusalem. He was 23 years old.

Krapf and Flad travelled to Ethiopia in 1855 and found the Emperor in Begemdir. They were impressed as they watched him distribute money to the poor and the lepers. The next day they were granted an audience. Unfortunately, Dr. Krapf, on the advice of Abuna Selama, did not tell the Emperor that the men that Bishop Gobat intended to send would be missionaries. The Abuna felt that this was his concern and, as Bishop, he would agree provided that the missionaries were not ordained and that all converts would be baptised into the Ethiopian Church. Krapf therefore stressed to the Emperor that the men would be artisans. Theodore agreed to give permits to a gunsmith, a builder, and an engraver, and that they would be free to hold meetings if the Abuna allowed it. No deception was intended, but when Flad returned the following year with three Chrischona brethren, they regarded themselves as primarily missionaries while the Emperor regarded them as primarily artisans.

Most Ethiopians and Europeans found the Abuna lazy, crooked and fond of money, and Flad was never happy with him. He could have played a big role in advancing God's work but he chose his own worldly enrichment instead, and it was sad to see him deteriorate. He knew he should have done something to educate the clergy, establish schools and reform the Church, but the effort needed and the cost deterred him.

In 1858 Flad suffered from severe toothache and was persuaded to go to Jerusalem for treatment at the C.M.J. Hospital. Deaconess Pauline Keller was in charge of the hospital pharmacy. She was the first woman in Europe to be a pharmacist and had shared a room for a short time during her training with Florence Nightingale. She was ready for adventure and danger in the service of Christ, and soon she and Flad became very close friends. They were married in 1858 and left for Ethiopia the day after the wedding, taking with them four more artisans. Their journey took them through the Sudan and their luggage, consisting mainly of Bibles in Amharic, was carried on thirty-three camels.

These journeys were adventurous and often dangerous as they had to sleep out in the open and sometimes saw the footprints of wild animals nearby the next morning. Once Flad woke up to find the leather bag he kept at his side at night was missing, and the next morning found that a hyena had taken the bag, emptying it of its contents as it went through the bush. On this journey two of the artisans died of cholera and sunstroke.

Bishop Gobat was able to give little money to his missionary artisans and it was intended that each should earn his living by his trade and by teaching it to the Ethiopians. When Flad reached Begemdir he found that the first three men had left the schools he had started there and stopped preaching. Lack of money had led them to offer their services to the Emperor, who set them to work building roads. They were allowed to hold meetings and to distribute Bibles, not without results, and the Emperor himself showed interest, but there was no doubt in his mind that the Kingdom of God could not be established by the Bible and preaching, a view which was shared by most of the Ethiopians.

The political plan seemed better

After his coronation Theodore continued the first part of his plan, to unite and reform Ethiopia, by conquering the King of Shewa, who died in the middle of the campaign. He returned to Gonder victorious in 1856 with Minilik, the son of the late King, as his prisoner.

Until then soldiers in Ethiopia had owed allegiance chiefly to their immediate superior, were undisciplined, and lived on the local population. Theodore intended to create a standing army with firearms only, and to convert swords and shields into ploughshares. He incorporated the soldiers he wanted into his own army, which he now paid, and sent the rest to plough their fields. Some were so used to living by robbery that they openly came to Theodore to say they could do nothing else. One group in Dembia refused his offer of more land in the plains below their village and started back to their homes in triumph. But they met some of the King's cavalry, who had been sent to teach them what he meant in the only way they could understand.

Meanwhile he gave much of his time to the administration of justice, which was fairer, though sometimes more severe, than the country had known for a very long time. He ate no food until he had finished this work in the middle of each afternoon. He abolished various vexatious Customs' charges, and intended to have only three customs posts in all his kingdom.

Feudalism was far from dead and the jealous sons of

Dejjazmach Kinfu, his own relatives, and those of Dejjazmach Wubey of Simeyn and other conquered rulers, stirred up revolts from 1857 to 1861. After defeating them all Theodore was supreme and undisturbed for some time. His first plan was well on the way to full success.

His second plan was to make the Christian faith dominant throughout the land, and with this aim he set a magnificent personal example from his coronation onwards for several years. He had married the daughter of the Galla ruler of Gonder in church, remained faithful to her and tried to get all around him to follow his example. After she died in 1858 to his great grief, he remained celibate until persuaded in 1860 that it was not wrong for a King like Theodore to marry again, and then he married (in church) the daughter of Dejjazmach Wubey.

He disdained luxuries, and often wore the clothes of an ordinary soldier. He was generous to the poor, the sick, and especially children. He suppressed the slave trade in his dominions as far as he could, and often bought slaves in order to baptize and free them. He did not know how to write, but he was so intelligent that he could dictate three letters at once. He tried to ally himself with Abuna Selama and to force all to accept the Bishop's views on doctrine. When he found some merchants in Gonder who had different views about the nature of Christ, he asked them if they acknowledged the Abuna. When they said "yes" he called in the executioner with his sword and told them they had better change their views or he would be given work to do. When they requested three days to think it over, he put them under guard without food or water, and was happy about their "conversion" as a result!

Abuna Selama was quite in agreement with such methods, but not with his proposals about Church management. Theodore wanted only two priests and three deacons allotted to each church and given enough Church land for their support; surplus priests were to plough their lands and pay taxes. Theodore tried persuasion, but by 1860 he was in such need of money for all his plans and battles that he forced this through. Many Ethiopians and foreigners commended him highly for so curbing the idleness and the number of the ignorant priests.

His third plan, to become the master of the world by defeating the Turks and capturing Jerusalem, had to start by the conquest of the Galla Moslems. In this he succeeded so quickly that some of his troops mutinied in Shewa in 1856, because they were afraid that he would immediately lead them to Jerusalem. He had seen enough of the Turks to know that he would need cannon and better disciplined troops before this could be achieved, and so he must be content to remain "the husband of Ethiopia and the fiancé of Jerusalem" for a while longer. The Turks had handed over control of Messawa and Suakim to Egypt in 1855 and 1856, but this made no difference to Theodore's plans, for both countries were Moslem.

He hoped that Bishop Gobat would help him by sending more artisans from Europe, and that Plowden would find others. But Plowden was captured by rebels, and although the people of Gonder paid the ransom demanded, he died of his wounds. Theodore gladly repaid the ransom money and wreaked vengeance on the rebels shortly afterwards. When Plowden's replacement, Captain Cameron, arrived in 1862 with gifts, he was well received and was considerably impressed. Theodore was then at the height of his power.

4

THE RISE OF A STAR

MARTIN FLAD reported to Bishop Gobat in 1858 that he found
a more encouraging response among the Felashas than among
the Amharas. When this report was sent to the Church's Ministry among the Jews it helped them to decide where to expand
the work still more.

There was a growing sympathy for the Jews amongst
Christians in England, and a still wider realisation that the
Church all over the world had maltreated them for many
centuries. Under the enthusiastic presidency of the Earl of
Shaftesbury, The Church's Ministry among the Jews became
one of the most popular of the missionary societies. It had
expanded its work from London to Palestine as well as to
most European and North African countries which had large
Jewish populations.

At its first Jubilee celebrations in 1859 the Society decided
to use the extra funds given that year to take the Gospel
to Jews in unreached areas. To test whether it was the will of
God for them to start a mission amongst the Felashas of
Abyssinia, as Ethiopia was then called in Europe, they sent
out the most courageous missionary on their staff, Henry
Aaron Stern.

Henry Aaron Stern

Stern, "a star" in German, was born to Jewish parents in
Germany in 1820 and brought up frugally. At the age of
nineteen he came to London to make his fortune, but a
fellow lodger took him to a service conducted by a C.M.J.
missionary, which began his interest in the New Testament.
This led to his conversion. He entered the C.M.J. Trade
School, and after that went on to their Missionary Training
School for two years. He was then sent to Jerusalem to serve
under Bishop Alexander, the first Anglican bishop there, who
was himself a converted Jew and a former C.M.J. missionary.
After being ordained by him he was sent to Baghdad and
Persia.

On his return to England in 1849 he was ordained priest

and married an English woman before returning to Persia the following year. A New Testament Stern gave to the Jewish Court Physician of the Shah, was read by the Physician's son Mirza Norollah, who after his conversion began what proved to be a very fruitful work among the Persian Jews, led until recently by Norollah's relations.

After Stern had been in charge of the work at Constantinople for three years, C.M.J. agreed in 1856 to his wish to be sent to Arabia. He travelled in Arab dress, and took the name of "The Dervish Abdulla". He made no attempt to hide his faith in Jesus Christ as he travelled with only a donkey driver to Senaa, the capital of the Yemen, in South Arabia, witnessing to all he met on the journey. In one town he had a letter of introduction to the Chief Rabbi, and all turned out to see this strange man who was dressed like a Moslem yet did not believe in the Koran, who had come to befriend the despised Jews and yet professed another creed. Only when he produced his books in Hebrew did they begin to believe his extraordinary story. But his presence caused resentment, and having been warned of plans to kill him he moved on to Senaa, where he found that out of a total population of 40,000 about 18,000 were Jews who claimed that their ancestors had gone there in the days of Nebuchadnezzar. Most of them were poor, fearful and hopeless, as they were robbed with virtual impunity by the Moslems and treated as second class citizens.

After Stern had spent twelve days at Senaa some Jews already professed conversion, and one or two Moslems were so much impressed that it became too dangerous both for him and for them to remain together any longer. A sheikh whom he had helped medically provided an escort, and though attacked on the way Stern reached Aden safely. There a ship's captain so admired his courage that he took him to Suez free. After a year's furlough in England he went back to Constantinople until called upon by C.M.J. in 1859 to test the prospects of starting a mission amongst the Felashas in Ethiopia.

The Start of the Mission

Stern reached Ethiopia in 1860, a year after Flad had returned from Jerusalem, and was granted an audience with King Theodore in May. As he had come purely as a missionary and not as an artisan the Emperor gave him permission to start a Mission among the Felashas, which was a great step forward. The Bishop agreed, provided all converts from among the Felashas were baptised into the Ethiopian Orthodox Church. Bishop Gobat still gave his artisan missionaries very little money for their work because he wanted them to live by their skill or trade, not realising to what extent a strong character like Theodore could force sincerely missionary-minded men to concentrate on their worldly skills and neglect their spiritual aims.

Stern made little attempt to hide his contempt for all the Emperor's 'workmen' as he called them, but Theodore honoured them as nobles at this time. Flad had started schools for the children at Gafat, near Debra Tabor, as he had done at Gonder, and it was here that Stern joined him. The artisans had built a furnace and a carpenter's shop there, and were building for the Emperor the first carriage in Ethiopia. Unwittingly Stern stirred up a lot of suspicion among the soldiers by taking photographs.

In September 1860, after the rainy season, Stern visited thirty Felasha villages with Flad as his interpreter. At first the Felashas refused to listen to them, but when they heard from Christian priests and soldiers that the beliefs of these missionaries were different from those commonly accepted in the Ethiopian Church their curiosity was aroused. They were surprised to find they were not being urged to idolatry, or the worship of Mary and the saints, as they had expected, but were pointed to the prophecies in their own Scriptures, and their fulfilment by Jesus Christ. The Felashas knew nothing of all this, for their priests read the Old Testament Scriptures to them in the dead language of Giiz, and rarely translated them.

Flad was unhappy about the work of the other artisans but showed it tactfully by quietly continuing with his schools and preaching the Gospel. Stern persuaded him to join in the work of C.M.J. and left him in charge when he went home to England in 1861 to report.

Bishop Gobat agreed to lend Flad to C.M.J. for a year, and together with two other missionaries he began to build

a station at Jenda, about fourteen miles north of Lake T'ana.
Again he started schools and preached among the many
Felashas living in nearby villages. The most learned of these
was a young man named Debtera Biru, who was destined to
become the first Felasha convert.

The First Convert

Debtera Biru was born in 1837 of a Felasha Jewish priest
who, by local standards, was well off, and the government
official in that area grew jealous and demanded to know by
what witchcraft he got his cattle to multiply. He was not
satisfied with the explanation that it was by the blessing of
the God of Israel, and the official fabricated an excuse for
putting him in chains and taking all his wealth. On release
the father took his weaving loom to Jenda, but later was
badly burnt when his hut caught fire, and he died shortly
afterwards. His widow kept her family by making pottery and
Biru started weaving from about the age of ten.

He was taught to read and write Amharic by a Christian
Debtera or learned man, and later taught himself Giiz and
learnt the Psalms by heart while weaving. He was soon able
to translate from Giiz to Amharic better than anyone else in
the area, and regularly translated the passage for the day
in the synagogue. Because of this the Felasha priests gave him
the title of Debtera.

Throughout 1861 he met with the missionaries, orginally
with the aim of discrediting them. But gradually he was
convinced that the offering of sacrifices was wrong, and that
many prophecies pointed to Jesus as the Messiah, the Saviour
of the world. Eventually, after a complete day of argument
between twenty Felashas and Flad he openly admitted that
these prophecies from their own holy books had convinced
him that Jesus was the Son of God. On the following Saturday
he told all in the synagogue that it was not the missionaries
but their own scriptures which had led him to this. He was
promptly beaten by those present and he and his supporters
were thrown out.

A few days later thirty Felasha priests and Debteras failed
to get him to turn back again, and they gave him eight days
in which to recant while threatening him with witchcraft.

After ten days he became very sick, and one morning Flad was summoned early as his relatives were convinced he was dying. Flad found him cold and stiff and prayed over him. Biru at last went to sleep, and when he woke two hours later he told his weeping mother that he would not die but live to preach the Gospel to the Felashas. It was with great joy that he and twenty others were baptized in July 1862, and the following month his mother and eighteen others were also received into the Ethiopian Church.

Now the arguments grew more and more fierce, especially about the sacrifices, until the Felashas appealed to the governor. Biru showed from the Bible why he preached that these should no longer be offered, and the controversy grew to such proportions that the governor told them all to go to the Emperor.

So some three hundred Felashas came to Theodore with many gifts, and Flad, Biru and other converts were there also with their Bibles. The leaders of the Felashas spoke first and Theodore, impressed by what they said, asked Flad by what authority he forbade the offering of the sacrifices. Flad said that he had given out 250 Bibles which had convinced forty Felashas that sacrifices were wrong, but that he had used no force or authority. Then the King questioned the converts and Biru answered humbly and well from the Bible. After consideration the King told them all to come again when the Abuna arrived. The Felashas took this as a judgment in their favour and went out with such rejoicing that the King was angered, recalled them, and forbade them to offer sacrifices from then on. In spite of one strong appeal a year later, they were forced to obey this until after his death. Meanwhile, Debtera Biru grew stronger spiritually and in the knowledge of God's Word and won many Felashas to his Lord.

The political plan no longer so popular

Theodore wanted to keep a larger army than the country's resources warranted, which led to increases in taxes. At the same time there were always some nobles who refused to accept his claim to be the Theodore of prophecy. Revolts increased in different parts of the country forcing him to permit plundering and atrocities in the rebellious areas. On one occasion he ordered the execution of 700 prisoners of war. By 1863 his first plan, uniting Ethiopia, seemed to be threatened and his second plan, making Ethiopia a wholly Christian country, was also failing. Theodore had lost the support of the Bishop and the Church by forcing so many priests to return to their farms, and many of them had joined the rebels.

The trouble was that he gave them more and more reason to doubt his divine appointment, for his former good and moral life had obviously deteriorated. His wife gave him no support and his times of fasting became very infrequent. He rarely prayed and never read the Bible now. He also ordered the artisans at Gafat to put aside all spiritual work and concentrate on making mortars and gunpowder. When they objected, he took away all financial support and threatened them with chains.

For his third plan, to conquer the Turks, Jerusalem and the world for Christ, he needed more artisans to make more mortars and gunpowder and appealed in 1862 to the French and the British. The former sent a non-committal answer, and the British put his letter into a file and forgot it. He began to suspect that the British were the allies of his enemies the Turks, especially when his messenger to the French, named Bardel, pointed out that the British had supported the Turks against the Russians in the Crimean war.

The final disappointment was the news that the Turks had expelled the Ethiopian monks from the part of the Church of the Holy Sepulchre which they had occupied for centuries, in spite of an appeal by Bishop Gobat to the British Consul there to try to prevent it. The monks put up simple huts on the roof of the Church of the Holy Sepulchre, where they have been ever since.

Hopes of dawn

Meanwhile, C.M.J. had been greatly encouraged by the reports sent home by Flad telling of conversions among the Felashas. They determined to send Stern out again to organise these converts the better, and he returned in April 1863 bringing with him a young man, Rosenthall, who like Stern himself was a Jewish convert married to an English Gentile wife. Stern, who was known in Ethiopia as "Kokeb", the Amharic for "Star", persuaded Flad to join C.M.J. fully, and Bishop Gobat agreed.

Flad was well educated but knew less English and was not ordained, which made Stern refer to him as Gobat's "Scripture Reader". Nevertheless the two men got on quite well together, and they made another big tour among Felasha villages in new areas, giving out more gospels and portions of Scripture, which Flad was specially keen on. Also he had begun to compose and translate tracts and booklets himself.

In just over a year sixty-five Felashas had been baptised and many more were known to be studying the Scriptures with interest. Many of these had been first drawn to the missionaries by the care and medical aid of Mrs. Flad. Martin Flad had commenced nine small schools for children in various villages near Jenda, and in addition to the teachers, employed four evangelists, one of whom was Biru.

By October 1863 Stern prepared to leave for England feeling that he had finished his work of organising the converts and the Mission, and could safely leave all to the leadership of Flad with high hopes for the future.

5

THE TWO PLANS CLASH

The first clash

STERN PROPOSED to journey to Messawa via Tigrey and took
two of Consul Cameron's servants who were from that territory as his guides. After the first day's travelling he found he
had pitched his tent quite near to the Emperor's camp.
Theodore was returning from an unsuccessful attempt to quell
a revolt and was consoling himself with drink. Not knowing
this, Stern thought to pay his respects to the Emperor, and
presented himself at the royal tent with the two servants as
his interpreters.

Neither Stern nor Consul Cameron enjoyed the confidence
of Theodore, who become suspicious when he realised that
the interpreters were servants of Consul Cameron. When one
dared to argue with the Emperor he ordered his guards to
beat them both to death in front of him. Stern was so horrified
that he put his thumb up to his mouth and bit it in his
anguish, not realising that this meant in Ethiopia "I will get
my revenge on you". At this gesture Theodore drew his own
pistol to shoot Stern, but thought better of it and ordered his
guards to beat him instead. This they did with such violence
that they thought they had killed him too. They dragged him
out of the tent, and left him bound to a guard.

Stern was made of tougher material than they realised, and
he eventually woke to full consciousness to find himself weak
from loss of blood and in great pain. He asked for water but
received a kick instead. Another more kindly soldier gave
him a drink, saying that his guard might pay for it with his
head if the hated foreigner died while in his charge.

The next day he was chained hand and foot and taken down
to Gonder, where Flad saw him and obtained permission to
look after him. Stern recovered, but it took three weeks. As
British Consul, Cameron pleaded for his release but the
Emperor reminded him of the unanswered letter. The Abuna
(bishop) added his plea, but he was no longer in the
Emperor's favour. However, the bitterest blow was caused by

Stern himself. Hearing that his belongings were being searched, he foolishly asked the Frenchman, Bardel, to bring him his confidential diary. This unscrupulous and ambitious character, with promotion in mind, took the diary to the Emperor. In his diary Stern had described the execution of the seven hundred followers of the Emperor's relations as "Cold blooded murder", and mentioned Theodore's humble birth and upbringing. When the diary was translated to the Emperor, he was understandably furious and put Stern in chains once again. Cameron and all the missionaries were arrested, their belongings ransacked and the houses burnt to the ground. Finally the Emperor ordered preparations for a public trial in Gonder in front of most of his troops, which then numbered more than 100,000.

The Trial

Theodore's aim in this trial was to discredit the Abuna and the priests as much as Stern and the English. He forced the priests to compose a genealogy proving that he was descended from Solomon. This was his first acknowledgment of the need to add anything to the list of his military successes to prove his claim to be the Theodore of prophecy.

At the trial Stern was distressed to see his colleague, Rosenthall, also in chains, because "still worse insults" had been discovered in his writings. Neither man asked for forgiveness, largely because they believed that the facts which they quoted were true. At the verdict Stern was acquitted of using the sign of revenge, as his ignorance was acknowledged, but he was condemned to death at a time to be decided later on the basis of his unauthorised photographs, and his disparaging remarks about the King and his European "workers", some of whom had married Ethiopian wives. Stern regarded himself as an English gentleman who must not demean himself by too much familiarity with the "natives", an attitude which a man of the ability and pride of Theodore had been previously quick to notice and resent.

The trial had been impressive, but it did not have the desired effect for long, and as Theodore gradually realised this he came to rely all the more upon the weapon he knew best, force and terror. In the background was the constant hope

THE TWO PLANS CLASH 45

that God would work miracles to vindicate His chosen
Theodore. This very dangerous belief that a man is fulfilling a
prophecy, or is a special tool of the Holy Spirit, can bring
him unconsciously to believe that he is temporarily above
the revealed laws of God. So Theodore became more and
more cruel, even to his own subjects, in order to fulfil his
idea of God's plan. Later he realised that a constantly
humbled Stern was of more use to him than a dead one, so
Stern was imprisoned, not executed.

Imprisonment

After the trial Mr. and Mrs. Flad had been forced to remain
in the camp of the King, guarded by soldiers, but eventually
the workers at Gafat prevailed upon him to free them and
allow them to go and live there. Letters were sent home occasionally, through converted Felashas, who took them at the
risk of their lives hidden in the amulets of a mule, or in a slit
in their stick, or sewn by Mrs. Flad into their clothes. During
these anxious days C.M.J. did all it could to gather prayer
support, and through its President, the Earl of Shaftesbury,
appealed to the British Government to help free the prisoners.
These had all been sent to Theodore's main Amba, or fortress,
at Mek'dela, where some of his friends were also for safety.

Conditions gradually eased in the prison there as the King
was mostly away elsewhere. Stern held daily prayers and many
Ethiopians were converted from amongst the prisoners and
soldiers; later a European Jew named Moritz Hall, a caster
in brass for the Emperor, was baptised. Flad re-started a
school at Gafat, composed tracts in Amharic, and did his best
to supply Stern and Rosenthall with money and food.
Rosenthall's wife joined him towards the end of their imprisonment, but his two little children died there, while Stern
became weaker in both body and mind.

In January 1864 the British Consul received a letter from the
Foreign Office ordering him to return to Messawa. There
were rumours at the time that the Turks, urged on by the
British, were preparing to attack Ethiopia, so when he asked
the Emperor for permission to leave, he too was put into
chains.

But internal troubles were soon to cause greater problems.

In 1864 and 1865 Shewa, Gojam, Tigrey, Lasta and even
North-west Begemdir all rebelled successfully against Theodore, leaving him with only the rest of Begemdir and the
country around his fortress of Mek'dela in Wello, to which
all prisoners were sent in November 1864. There Stern and
Cameron were packed into the common prison which was
so full that the prisoners did not have room even to stretch
out on the ground.

When the news of Cameron's imprisonment reached
England, a special envoy named Rassam, an experienced
diplomat, was sent to Ethiopia with a letter from Queen
Victoria. He arrived at Messawa in June 1864, but the
Emperor was fully occupied with rebellions in various parts
of the country and did not see Rassam until January 1866.
Queen Victoria's letter brought by Rassam was badly translated and gave Theodore the impression that Rassam would
stay as an adviser when the prisoners were released. On this
assumption the missionaries and artisans were released, but
were arrested again when Rassam presented himself before the
Emperor to say goodbye. Another mock trial was arranged,
not nearly so grand as the previous one, for Theodore's army
was now down to only about 25,000 men.

New work for the Flads

The Emperor felt that the best way to get the artisans he
so desperately needed was to keep Rassam as a hostage and
send Flad to Queen Victoria with a clear demand for more
artisans. He trusted Flad but said he would keep in Ethiopia
"his heart and two eyes", meaning Mrs. Flad and the two
children. (See photographs for Theodore's letter).

Martin Flad was received in audience by Queen Victoria
twice, and the British Government took a very serious view
of the situation, realising it could mean ultimately an invasion
of Ethiopia. Flad returned to Ethiopia a year later in April
1867 with a kind but firm letter from the Queen demanding
the release of the prisoners, who were to be exchanged for
seven artisans in Messawa. Theodore then said he would only
release them when the artisans reached him, and Rassam
advised the Foreign Office to comply with the Emperor's
request, but before the letter reached the Foreign Secretary,

Lord Stanley, he had lost patience and ordered the artisans home. A full-scale invasion was then begun to be planned.

Meanwhile, Mrs. Flad and the children were lodged with the army in a large hut near the shore of Lake T'ana, which had been occupied by soldiers. Their first night was sleepless, and next morning the bed was put into the lake and the hut thoroughly cleaned to get rid of the fleas and bed bugs. Later, the loss of three sheep led her to discover that two leopards had been living in the huge thatched roof. After that cholera swept the area and the whole army moved up from Lake T'ana, at 6,000 feet, to the much colder Debra Tabor and Gafat at 9,000 feet. Mrs. Flad was given a tent, but later moved to a small house in the compound of one of the iron workers. She had to keep some mules, for she never knew when the Emperor would order them to go somewhere else, and she was also allowed to keep her servants, which was a great blessing with so many around her needing help. Rassam had helped as much as he could, but in July he had been sent to join the other prisoners at Mek'dela where they were reasonably well treated except that they were chained. Once the Emperor sent her six bales of cloth with orders to teach his tailors how to make from them as many shirts as possible. He paid her well for doing it, and she shared the money with Mrs. Rosenthall.

The general situation was becoming serious. No seed remained for sowing, there were no cattle with which to plough, and much of the province was becoming like a desert. The people also suffered from plundering by the soldiers, and Mrs. Flad was very distressed when Biru and other Felasha converts visited her dressed in rags. She ministered to these also and shared with them what little she had.

In January two Scottish missionaries planned with Bardel to escape, but he informed the Emperor of their intentions. He promptly put them in chains and sent soldiers to see if Mrs. Flad was implicated. They pushed into her house and found her in bed!

By 1867 it was clear to almost all that the King was not the Theodore of prophecy after all, and some said he was mad or demon possessed. The people of Begemdir were too poor to pay their taxes and were treated as rebels. Whole villages

were burnt, sometimes with the inhabitants purposely barred
in. Theodore was so suspicious of everyone that to be too
successful in his service was as unwise as to be a failure.
Most Ethiopians were fatalistic about it all; "if we had not
been so wicked God would not have given us so cruel a
King", they said.

When Flad returned in April he gave the Emperor, together
with the Queen's letter, an oral message to the effect that if
he did not free the prisoners Britain would declare war, but
by this time Theodore was past caring. He needed his European artisans who were making bigger and bigger carriages
for the mortars they had built, and were blasting out roads
to transport them. In spite of this some of his advisers wanted
the Europeans killed, and all of them, especially the missionaries and the prisoners, realised the possibility that any day
their execution might be ordered. Flad was forced to help
the artisans, and because the Emperor knew he hated such
work he put him in chains for a few days to give him a taste
of the alternative.

Frustrated hopes

Theodore had relied upon the Abuna Selama at the
beginning to be his chief help in the spiritual side of his
plans, but lost the Abuna's support when he cut down the
number of clergy and so the Abuna's income. In 1864 the
Emperor confined him in the fortress of Mek'dela. One of the
Abuna's efforts to continue his duties as the one and only
bishop was to fill a leather bag with his breath, and several
men were considered to have been ordained priests after taking
a whiff of this 'holy breath'. The Abuna died at Mek'dela at
the early age of 47, it is said not so much from ill treatment,
as from too much drink and opium, and leading an irregular
life.

Rassam and the missionaries had sometimes hoped that the
rebels would capture Mek'dela during one of the Emperor's
absences, but it was well fortified and the rebels were not
united. They thought of trying to escape but were deterred
by the fact that the women and children and other friends
were under the power of Theodore at Gafat, near Debra
Tabor. Rassam obviously admired the Emperor and seemed

to be deceived by his friendly letters, but there was no other human leader to whom they could look. But the missionaries were greatly helped by the knowledge that God had been calling forth massive prayer support from Christians all over England and in many parts of Europe. Their confidence in God's ability to deliver them had been built up during the years of imprisonment by many examples of it. Those at Mek'dela especially were often terribly bitten by bugs and fleas, and were always in danger of disease and sometimes of starvation. But their messengers proved faithful, and money or food always reached them in time. When the Emperor was at Mek'dela the missionaries feared each day for their lives. Theodore on one occasion told Flad himself that he had intended to kill him but that God had restrained him. Most of the time he was away fighting the rebels and discipline was always relaxed when he left. Sometimes they had the joy of seeing God's Spirit at work in further conversions. There were also more Ethiopians there who had married their wives in Church than in any other town in the land, again chiefly because of the witness of the missionaries.

Mrs. Flad was sometimes down to her last dollar or her last pound or two of flour, but never was she allowed to go without. The Lord provided in time through the artisans at Gafat, or through some Ethiopian who had received a kindness before. Once they had almost nothing left when an Ethiopian brought them 80 dollars, and asked for a letter to the Consul at Messawa to repay him and to give him work, so that he might escape both the horrors of life under Theodore and the robbers on the way.

6

THE BATTLE OF MEK'DELA

Two roads to Mek'dela

THEODORE WAS making a road from the temporary capital at
Debra Tabor to Mek'dela, a distance of about 80 miles over
very rough and mountainous country. The road had to be
made wide enough for mortars of up to seven tons, and in
parts had ascents or descents of up to 3,000 feet. It was
exacting work for the remaining 10,000 soldiers. The Europeans had to supervise the work, and the missionaries, including the Flad family, had to accompany this ever-moving host
of workers. Only one with the indomitable will and energy of
Theodore could have kept the men at such an exhausting
task. Once he stood on a rock and glowered down at the
sweating soldiers and workers, and said: "I know you all
hate me, but here I stand, one man, and you are thousands!
Why do you not kill me?" When they gave no answer he
shouted, "Well, I will kill you all one by one. Go on with
your work." They obeyed—with admiration!

A month after starting the road Theodore heard that the
British had landed at Zula to the south of Messawa. He was
quite unperturbed, saying he looked forward to seeing a
disciplined European army, and seemed to think it would
somehow restore his fortunes. He told the artisans that there
was an Ethiopian legend that a great European king would
meet with a great Ethiopian one, and they would settle the
affairs of the land together. Theodore's troops looked like
vagabonds, as did the artisans and the missionaries. They
had no beds, and often insufficient water and wood. The Flads
managed to keep up with the rest in spite of the children
catching measles, being hot and thirsty by day and cold at
night, with frosts on the higher regions.

The British troops had a rough and difficult road of four
hundred miles to Mek'dela, and their equipment included
artillery carried by forty elephants. The main force from
India landed in February 1868. To the prisoners' great disappointment their arrival had been delayed, as they had

prepared for a hostile journey from the coast to Mek'dela. As it turned out, the ruler of Tigrey was as anxious as the British to overthrow the Emperor, and the British forces were welcomed by the inhabitants as liberators from a tyrant. Sir Robert Napier underlined this by proclaiming that it was his intention to release the prisoners and not to annex any terri- tory. All supplies needed locally were paid for by Maria Theresa dollars specially minted for the expedition.

The King and his mortars did not reach Mek'dela until the end of March. By that time his kingdom was little more than that huge amba or fortress on a three-headed mountain ridge, about three quarters of a mile long by about half a mile wide, rising 1,000 feet above the surrounding plain with only one good practicable path up to it. On this plateau was the palace and treasury, a Church, and nearly 3,000 huts, with an average now of about ten people per hut.

Theodore had not been seen by the prisoners at Mek'dela for nearly two years and he looked ten years older than his fifty years. Desertions, due to his cruelties on the way to Mek'dela, had reduced his army to 7,000 men. Two weeks later the British arrived with a force of 4,000.

The Battle

On Palm Sunday, 5th April 1868, a prisoner recklessly insulted the Emperor who, to strengthen discipline before the coming battle, ordered nearly two hunderd prisoners to be beaten to death and their bodies thrown over the cliffs. He spent most of the following night alternately drinking and praying for forgiveness.

As Sir Robert Napier approached Mek'dela on the following Thursday, he sent out a party to reconnoitre. The officer who led this party was a true Christian, who never failed to have a quiet time of prayer and Bible reading each morning. He got up very early on Good Friday, 10th April, and asked God to guide him to the best way of freeing the prisoners. When he got nearer to Mek'dela he could see it was so strong that he doubted if the whole British force could ever take it. In the afternoon, to his amazement, he saw the gates of the fort open and the Ethiopian soldiers come streaming down. He immediately sent a runner to report to Sir Robert Napier, trusting that this was God's answer to the prayers of so many.

Theodore, with little information about the British force, may have thought either that the advance guard was the whole British force, or could be wiped out before others were able to come to their help. The battle raged the rest of the day with 2,000 British troops involved against 4,000 poorly armed Ethiopians. The Ethiopian soldiers fought magnificently but many had only spears and shields, and the rest had only muzzle loading rifles, which were seriously affected by a thunder storm in the middle of the battle. In spite of this the Ethiopian soldiers reformed and charged again and again until nightfall. Over 700 of them were killed and 1500 wounded while the British casualties were twenty wounded of whom only two later died.

Answers to many prayers

At the end of the day, when Theodore and the remaining troops came back to his fortress, all the prisoners feared greatly that he would now command their execution. Instead of this he asked their advice and even followed it. The next morning at dawn he sent his son-in-law with Martin Flad to ask Sir Robert Napier what were his terms for peace. Sir Robert showed the Emperor's son-in-law all his artillery and rockets, most of which had not got to the scene of action in time for the battle. Sir Robert sent back a letter through them saying that Theodore had fought well but that he must free all the prisoners and that he and his family would be given "honourable treatment." Theodore refused to keep the letter and gave it to Flad. It is still treasured by the Flad family. In his reply to Sir Robert, the Emperor, in accepting the peace terms, showed his better nature. He hoped honourable treatment meant caring for the many women and widows he had supported in a mainly heathen country. He complained that his troops were not as well trained as the British, and darkness had prevented his rallying them, as he had done so successfully on previous occasions. He had planned to free Jerusalem from the Turks and conquer the world, but if this was not possible he would prefer to die. His people had now turned against him, but "out of what evil I have done towards them may God bring good".

The missionaries had been wonderfully protected in answer to prayer. Only on the previous Thursday Theodore had ordered the execution of all the European prisoners, when an Ethiopian noble said that they ought not to die an easy death but be burnt alive in a specially built hut. The Emperor agreed, and the execution was put off while the hut was being built. But on Good Friday he went to the Church, and saw a picture of the Crucifixion of Christ. From then until his end he was much more merciful.

As Flad left again for the British lines with this letter, the Europeans who were still with him saw Theodore get up suddenly and pray, bow down three times and then take his pistol to kill himself. One noble quickly grabbed it and the bullet only nicked his ear. Another noble reminded him of the order to burn the Europeans but the Emperor said No! and asked how he could stand before God with their blood on his hands. There is little doubt as to what would have happened if he had succeeded in killing himself then. His son-in-law advised him instead to release the prisoners, to which the Emperor readily agreed. When the prisoners were being led away they thought they were being taken to their deaths. They could not believe that they were really being released until they reached the British camp. They met Flad on his way to the fortress with a verbal message that all must be released, for Mrs Flad and the artisans were still in the fortress. On Sunday Theodore sent a gift of 500 sheep and 1,000 cattle, as it was Easter Day. When it was reported (erroneously as it turned out) that this gift had been accepted Theodore freed the rest of the Europeans. Three times had Flad put himself into the power of the lion again and now thanking God he led his wife and children away to safety. When they reached the British camp there was a great service of thanksgiving, at which the preacher was the prisoner who had had to endure more than any other man for four and a half years, the converted Jew, Henry Aaron Stern. At the suggestion of the Archbishop of Canterbury services of thanksgiving were held in all part of the British Empire.

Theodore dismissed his army, and left Mek'dela with a few devoted followers. He found that he was too hemmed in by Galla enemies to be able to escape, and so he returned, preferring to die defending the fortress against the British, who bombarded it on Easter Monday for two hours.

Just before the final attack, after Theodore had been wounded, he said to his arms-bearer, "I believed hitherto that God was with me, and I thought I was fulfilling His will in all that I did. I now see that it was not God, but the devil, who was with me, and urging me to be so cruel". Then he shot himself.

God had delivered Ethiopia of a gifted emperor, who had caused almost all to hate him as a tyrant, and He had freed 91 Ethiopians, 59 Europeans, and 8 others from death at his hands time and again in answer to the prayers of thousands. The main battle had been fought and won in the spiritual realm, as many Ethiopians there realised, for they said to the last prisoners as they left, "Your God is a mighty God".

Freedom

When Sir Robert Napier addressed his troops later, he said "Our complete and rapid success is due, firstly, to the mercy of God whose hand, I feel assured, has been over us in a just cause." This mercy was to be seen in the fact that only two British soldiers died of their wounds and two or three of sickness during the whole campaign.

Very little was found at Mek'dela except one crown which was later given back to Ethiopia; the seal, and most of the manuscripts and other treasures taken from the churches of Gonder. Theodore was buried at the church at Mek'dela near the grave of Abuna Selama, and the rest of the fortress was burnt. The British had kept their word and paid the whole cost of the expedition, while Ethiopia had been given her freedom.

On the 15th April the British force started on the long road back. About a week later Mrs. Flad gave birth to a little girl, whom they named "Arinnetey", the Amharic for "My Freedom". The whole army stopped for one day to allow her to recover before taking her on by mule and litter.

Sir Robert was given the title of Lord Napier of Magdala by Queen Victoria, who honoured him by attending a huge reception at the Crystal Palace, London. Mr. and Mrs. Flad had bought some reasonably good clothes for the occasion, but even so they were obviously not nobility. When they tried to enter, the usher doubted even their written invitation and kept them waiting for a long time. To his consternation he saw them conducted to seats next to the Queen and Lord Napier.

This noble soldier sought on this and every other occasion to give God the glory for that wonderful deliverance. At a banquet in Edinburgh he concluded his speech with these words, "Never have I conducted a more difficult, never a more successful campaign than the one to Abyssinia. It is not my merit that all Europeans were brought out safely, it was in answer to the many thousands of prayers that were sent up to Almighty God that it was done. I was but the instrument in God's hand."

7

BOTH PLANS RESUMED AND RESISTED

Resumed abroad

The Battle of Mek'dela had put Ethiopia on the map as far as the European powers were concerned, and her importance grew with the construction of the Suez Canal.

Flad had thought to study for a while before working among the Jews somewhere in Europe, but C.M.J. asked him and Mrs. Flad to return to Ethiopia. They were horrified at the prospect, but after much prayer they saw clearly that it was God's will that they should try to do so, although no other missionary offered to accompany them. Stern had never intended to return in any case, nor would his health have permitted it. In 1871 he became Senior Missionary in charge of all the C.M.J. institutions in London, and in 1885 he died at the age of 65.

During his visit to England in 1866 Flad had met a Mrs. Potts, who had been converted through one of the secretaries of C.M.J. God gave her a deep concern for the work among the Felashas, and she offered to help with the training of some of the Felasha converts. This enabled Flad to send four of them to his own former Bible School at St. Chrischona.

Flad worked among the Jews in Germany in the summers and translated books into Amharic or composed tracts in the winters. Mrs. Potts paid for the printing of these, and in 1870 took over the financial support of the whole Mission. At the end of that year Flad left his wife and the children with Dr. Krapf and set out on his fifth journey to Ethiopia. He stayed with Swedish missionaries who had recently settled near Messawa, and then went through the Sudan on to Metemma with twenty-four camels loaded with Bibles, books and tracts. The books included copies of "Man's Heart" and also Dr. Barth's Bible stories, which Flad had translated and shown to the Emperor Theodore, who had liked it so much that he had kept the manuscript, and so Flad had to translate it all over again.

1. The foothills of the Simeyn mountains.

2. A Felasha village. The hut in the left foreground is for the ceremonially unclean who may not go beyond the line of stones.

3. A Jewish priest and his son come to the clinic at Jenda.

4. Another Felasha Jewish priest, K'es Asris, and his wife, after their conversion to Christ.

British Camp Afeejoo
11th April 1868

Your Majesty has fought like a brave man, and has been overcome by the superior power of the British Army.

It is my desire that no more blood may be shed.

If therefore your Majesty will submit to the Queen of England, and bring all the European[s] now in your Majesty's hands, and deliver them safely this day in the British camp, I guarantee honourable treatment for yourself and all the members of your Majesty's Family —

R Napier General
Commander in Chief

5. Letter of Sir Robert Napier taken to King Theodore by Martin Flad after the battle of Magdala in 1868.

በስመ ፡ አብ ፡ ወወ ልድ ፡ ወመንፈስ ፡ ቅዱስ ፡
፩ አምላክ ፡፡ የእግዚአብሔር ፡ ፍጡር ፡ ባር ያ
ው ፡ የዳዊት ፡ የሰሉ ሎሞን ፡ ልጅ ፡ ንጉሠ ፡ ነገ ሥ ተ ፡ ኢ ዮጵያ ፡ ቴዎ ድሮስ ፡፡ ዘ ኢ ት ዮ ጵ ያ ፡፡ እቶ ፡
ፍ ላ ጥ ን ፡ በ እ ዴ ሮ ጳ ፡ ል ኬ ፡ ሰ ድ ጀ ዋ ለ ሁ ፡፡ ብ
ል ህ ፡ ሠ ራ ተ ኛ ፡ ፈ ል ጌ እ ለ ሁ ፡፡ ከ ኔ ፡ የ ሚ ወ ጣ
ን ፡ ሠ ራ ተ ኛ ፡ ሁ ሉ ፡ በ ደ ስ ታ ፡ እ ቀ በ ለ ዋ ለ ሁ ፡
ቢ ኖ ር ም ፡ ደ ስ ፡ እ ስ ኘ ች ፡ እ ና ረ ዋ ለ ሁ ፡፡ ብ
ል ሀ ቱ ን ይ ም ፡ አ ስ ተ ም ሬ ፡ ወ ደ አ ገ ሬ ፡ እ መ ለ
ሰ ለ ሁ ፡ ዲ ላ ፡ ደ መ ወ ዙ ን ፡ ሠ ጥ ቼ ፡ ደ ስ ፡ እ
ስ ኘ ች ፡ ሽ ኘ ች ፡ እ ሰ ደ ዋ ለ ሁ ፡፡ በ እ ግ ዚ አ ብ ሔ
ር ፡ ኃ ደ ል ፡፡ የ እ ግ ዚ አ ብ ሔ ር ፡ እ ም ነ ት ደ ሁ ነ በ ኝ ፡፡

ክ ር ስ ቶ ስ ፡ በ ተ ወ ለ ደ ፡ በ ኀ ህ ፡ ተ ፲ ፰ ፻ ፶ ፰ ዘ መ
ን ፡ በ ዘ መ ነ ፡ ማ ር ቆ ስ ፡ በ ሚ ዝ ያ ፡ በ ፲ ቀ ን ፡ ዘ ጌ ፡
ላ ይ ፡፡ ተ ጻ ፈ ፡፡

6. Letter of King Theodore in Amharic taken to England by Martin Flad in 1866.

Translation:— ''In the name of the Father, the Son, and the Holy Spirit, One God. The creature and slave of God, the son of David and Solomon, the King of Kings of Ethiopia, Theodore. I have sent Mr. Flad via Europe. I have wanted clever artisans. I will receive each artisan who comes to me. If he wishes to remain I will cause him to dwell happily. If he says I will teach my trade and then return to my country, I will pay him his wages and send him on his way rejoicing. By the power of God, may God's faithfulness be found in me.

Written at Zegey (on Lake T'ana) on the 10th of Miyazya (April) in the year of St. Mark, 1858 (Ethiopian Calendar=1866 European Calendar) years after the birth of Christ''. Seal of King Theodore.

Resumed in Ethiopia

From Metemma Flad sent a message to the nearest ruler, who advised him not to go further as all Ethiopia was too unsettled, so he stayed in the heat of Metemma for three months. Many Ethiopians risked a long journey to buy books from him there.

Biru had written the year before to say he had been able to witness to very many Felashas. He was obviously the leader of the converts, and was now re-employed with two or three others.

Flad returned to Germany where he found little response among the Jews and was once in danger of his life through them. He put more books through the printing press at St. Chrischona including the Psalter in Amharic and Giiz. In 1873 one of the students there died and the doctor said that another might also die if he were to stay in Europe. Flad took the ailing student and three others back to Ethiopia reaching Metemma in December with the usual camel train of Bibles and literature.   Much depended on these four students for the future development of the work.

Aregawi was twenty-five years of age. He was the only Amhara, the others were Felashas. He lost his mother when he was three, and his father left him with Flad later to become a monk. His courage meant much to Mrs. Flad, especially during the burning of the Mission in 1863 when he was 14. Consul Cameron paid his fare to Europe to be educated three years later, when Flad was sent by Theodore to Europe. After three years at an orphanage in Germany he went to St. Chrischona, where he successfully completed his course of training while acting as interpreter to the other Ethiopian students.

Agashey was twenty-two years old. His mother died soon after he was born and his father gave him to the Felasha monks. As he grew up he became disillusioned by their frequent quarrels about money and property and left them to join the small mission school at Jenda, where he was converted and baptized in 1862. He was one of Mrs. Flad's helpers during the difficult years of imprisonment and was taken to Egypt after the fall of Mek'dela. He became a servant and finally was sent to St. Chrischona in 1870. Although the least clever of the four, this young man seemed to be the most spiritual.

Semani was twenty-three, and became a weaver at Jenda when he was ten years old to help support his widowed mother and family. He too was converted and baptised in 1862 and attended the school run by Biru. He ran away when he thought all the Europeans were going to be killed, and became the servant of a British officer. Later at Messawa European Jews tried, unsuccessfully, to get him to renounce his faith. After being recommended by the missionaries at Messawa, he was sent to St. Chrischona in 1870. He was a mild and humble young man of delicate health.

Senbetu, his younger brother, also attended the school at Jenda, and was employed as a servant by one of the artisans. Taken by him to Jerusalem he attended Bishop Gobat's school for three years, and, on the Bishop's recommendation, was sent to St. Chrischona in 1871. His eyesight was bad and he was unable to complete his training to be either an evangelist or a teacher.

Resisted everywhere

The British, when they left Ethiopia, gave a lot of arms to the ruler of Tigrey. These enabled him to establish an ascendancy over the other rulers, and he was crowned Emperor in 1872, taking the throne name of John IV. Flad now wrote asking for permission to return to his work in Ethiopia with these four young men, saying he had a letter from Queen Victoria.

During the six weeks Flad had to wait in Metemma for the Emperor's answer his precious baggage of Bibles was three times endangered by fire. The Emperor replied that he would be glad to receive the Queen's letter, but he would allow only the Copts of Egypt as religious teachers in Ethiopia. He had applied to the Coptic Patriarch in Egypt for a successor to the late Abuna Selama, and a new Abuna had been sent on condition that the Emperor sent away all missionaries. So Flad set out from Metemma with a heavy heart, but when he reached Jenda he was very cheered to witness the baptism of Agashey's uncle, who, twelve years before, had strongly opposed his nephew's baptism.

Flad travelled on to the Emperor's camp in Gojam and approached him through long lines of soldiers. The Emperor was glad to receive the Queen's letter and the literature Flad gave him, but, being a Tigrey whose language was more like Giiz, he was not too happy about the Psalter in Amharic. The Emperor, a fanatical member of the Ethiopian Church, was anxious to keep on friendly terms with the new Abuna and gave Flad only twenty days to reorganise the Mission at Jenda under the leadership of Biru and the four young men. Mrs. Potts had been rightly led to pay for the training of these four young Ethiopians of very humble origin.

Among the messages Flad brought to the Emperor was an offer of trade from the Viceroy of Egypt, but he said he wanted no friendship with Moslems, because when he had won full control of Ethiopia he was going to attack Egypt and free Jerusalem. The political plan had evidently been revived also.

When he got back to Jenda Flad organised the Mission, including the two remaining schools, under the leadership of Biru, who would have eleven others to assist him, and before he left he had the joy of witnessing the baptism of two former Felasha priests. On the nineteenth day a detachment of soldiers arrived to make sure that he left for the very difficult journey through Begemdir and Tigrey to Messawa.

The Viceroy of Egypt, imagining that Lord Napier had had an easy victory, attacked Ethiopia twice in 1875 and 1876, but both attacks were unsuccessful.

The Governor of Messawa was murdered in 1875 because of his efforts to suppress the slave trade, and in 1876 Ismail Pasha of Egypt offered Flad the governorship of the three provinces of Messawa, Kassala and Suakim on the Red Sea. Flad asked for time to consult Bishop Gobat, Dr. Krapf and C.M.J. The Bishop and Krapf were inclined to advise acceptance, while C.M.J. was uncertain and felt it was best for Flad himself to seek for God's guidance on this matter. Flad's governorship would probably make for better relations between Egypt and Ethiopia, but what of the effect on the work of the Mission? Which plan would Flad favour for the good of Ethiopia, the political or the spiritual one? He finally became convinced that if he accepted the governorship it would

be interpreted in Ethiopia as going over to the Moslems,
and the evangelists and converts would probably be
imprisoned and perhaps killed. He decided not to accept.
When he told the evangelists later on, they praised God for
this decision, and confirmed that the fears he had were
certainly well founded. Had he given in to the temptation to
use power and wealth to fulfil God's plans it may well have
meant ruin for the Mission. He had been led to see that
spiritual and not worldly power was the better way.

Force and death versus faith and the Bible

When Flad left Jenda with the soldiers the evangelists knew
that they were facing hardship and perhaps persecution, and
soon after the ruler of Dembia ordered them to stop preaching
and teaching, but they chose to obey God rather than men.
The priests incited neighbours more than once to assemble at
night to burn their houses, but God prevented this. The
Emperor had cut off all communication with Messawa so
there were no letters to or from Flad. Aregawi and Agashey
put on old clothes and made for the border by unfrequented
ways, but were caught by a detachment of soldiers. They fell
on their knees and prayed, fearing that they would have their
hands and feet cut off, and then they gave all their money to
the soldiers, who then set them free.

The Emperor John, after defeating the Egyptians, relied
still more on force and the power of the Ethiopian Church
as his chief means of uniting Ethiopia. He ordered all
K'imants and all Moslems, including Moslem rulers, to be
baptised and live outwardly as Christians, and it was his
intension to extend this order to include the Felashas. The
houses of the evangelists were often plundered by the soldiers
and any Bibles which they found were burnt, but the evangelists continued to preach and teach. One of them, Semani,
was taken seriously ill after three years of such faithful
witnessing, during which several Felashas had turned to
Christ. He had a coffin made which he kept by his bedside,
telling his visitors that he did not fear death, and urging the
Christians to witness with boldness. When he died in 1878
the priests thought so highly of him that they buried him in
ground previously reserved for bishops. Shortly afterwards

Agashey contracted smallpox from a convert he was visiting and died calling on the soul of Semani to wait for him.

General Gordon of Khartoum tried to make a treaty of peace with King John in 1879, but by the end of the year the King had already declared war on Egypt. He still aimed at capturing Jerusalem.

Flad wrote regularly hoping that some of his letters would get through, and in 1880 arranged for another conference at Metemma. It was as usual a testing journey, with the great variations in temperature, and riding a camel for eight hours each day until all his bones ached. One day they passed a band of robbers and Flad quietened the camel keepers by telling them he was a friend of God and was not afraid. At night he ordered the camp to be pitched in an open spot and himself acted as guard. When he heard voices during the night he fired his revolver in the air in that direction and the robbers went off. Two days later the same robbers attacked a caravan and killed two men. When Flad's party reached the other side of Kassala they found so many wild animals that they were forced to stay at wayside hotels, but the bed bugs and the smells made life miserable each night. With three men to guard against crocodiles it was a joy to have a good bath in the river.

When Flad reached Metemma in January 1881, just after his fiftieth birthday, he found that all Ethiopians had been forbidden to go to Metemma, so he sent a messenger to the evangelists with a letter to the Emperor. He received a reply from them in February saying that Biru and Aregawi dared not risk visiting Metemma nor had they dared to send Flad's letter on to the Emperor. They suggested that he should write direct to the Emperor asking for permission to enter, but C.M.J. had strictly forbidden this. However, the Word of God is not bound, and if Flad could not get into Ethiopia God had made provision for the Bibles to reach the evangelists. Eleven camels had arrived at Metemma from King John to take back corrugated iron for churches and his own palace, so Flad sent his camels with them.

The Emperor John allowed the boxes of literature to be delivered to Jenda. This unexpected blessing prompted the evangelists, realising that there was no hope of Flad coming back, to take on more responsibility, especially in Gojam, where the ruler had turned to Christ through the book "Man's Heart". By this time there had been at least 800 baptisms amongst the Felashas.

Soon after Flad left Metemma the Mahdi in the Sudan revolted, and in 1883 Britain withdrew completely from the country, making journeys to Ethiopia much more difficult. Flad's only contact was by those letters which got through. There was some loss of enthusiasm by 1885, and there was grumbling about Biru and the small pay the evangelists received. Flad himself revised the Amharic Bible for the Bible Society. In 1885 he suggested, not for the first time, that the Mission be closed, and when C.M.J. urged him to continue he suggested that Aregawi should come to Europe for a while and then return to put new life into the evangelists. Aregawi travelled to Germany by way of Egypt, and when he got to Alexandria he was so glad to be on his way that he gave himself a carriage ride as a treat. The driver asked him where he wanted to go and he just said "straight on". Each time the driver enquired he was given the same answer until he thought he was mad and said so. By this time Aregawi thought it best to tell him to go back. At the end he offered the man two piastres and was told that the price was ten. He paid it but was so mortified by this "expensive spree" that he fasted for four days, eating only potatoes and drinking coffee.

When Aregawi reached Flad they went together to England and stayed for a few days with Mrs. Potts; only after he had left did she discover that Aregawi had slept on the carpet. He had slept in beds before, of course, but he felt he would only spoil himself for Ethiopia if he slept in such a beautiful one. London he likened to the anteroom of Paradise, but he loved the Bible so much that he said that of all the sights in London the Bible Society's headquarters, with its many, many Bibles was the best.

In the summer he helped Flad with the revising of the Amharic Bible, and returned to Ethiopia in October to find the Emperor was again showing his opposition to the Mission. He was accused of leaving the country without permission, the priests of Gonder denounced him as a Protestant, and the Mayor, stripping him of most of his clothes, imprisoned him in a damp dungeon where he wished he would die. It was a fortnight before his colleagues were able to persuade the Mayor to release him.

It was encouraging that Aregawi and the other evangelists continued to witness under such conditions and that Flad was able to lead the Mission with such slender contacts. For three years Flad had no news from Ethiopia at all for the province of Begemdir was going through a very hard time.

8

STRONG OPPOSITION

Mahdists versus Martyrs

THE EVANGELISTS in Ethiopia had only two doors to the outside world, via Messawa and the Red Sea, or via Metemma and the Sudan. Now both doors were closed, for the British and Egyptians withdrew from the Sudan and Messawa after General Gordon's death at Khartoum at the hands of the Mahdists in 1884, and the Italians occupied Messawa in 1885. There was constant fighting between the Italians and King John who forbad Ethiopians to go to Eritrea. In 1886 the Mahdists, fanatical Moslem dervishes, wishing to avenge previous defeats, invaded western Ethiopia from the Sudan, and penetrated beyond Gonder to Debra Tabor, where they were held, but not defeated until two years later. In their advance they burnt all churches and most of the villages including Jenda. When they captured Jenda Aregawi's wife was with child, so she begged him to flee to a cave while she concealed herself as best she could in a hollow. Neither was discovered and they were able to escape eastwards. There a little son was born to them amidst great hardship.

Thirty families of the Felasha converts were not so fortunate. They were caught by the Dervishes and ordered to become Moslem. All refused and all became martyrs. A fifty-three year old Felasha convert was seized with his wife and five children, who were told they could save their lives by repeating the short Moslem creed, "There is but one God, and Mohammed is his prophet", but this meant denying Christ and they refused. They tried to persuade the father by compelling him to watch while his wife and children were killed, but he encouraged each to stand firm. Then they gave him a last chance to save himself: "Now, old dog, save your life and become a Muslim. We will make you a rich man and give you all you wish". But he shouted at his captors, "You may torture me, you may cut me to pieces, but I will not deny Him Who died for me". A dozen sword thrusts made him another willing martyr. Clearly the Felasha converts were able to become very fine Christians, and showed that the Mission was well worth while.

In 1889 the Emperor John attacked and defeated the dervish army at Metemma after they had been driven off the plateau the year before, but at the end of the battle he himself was killed. Fortunately for Ethiopia, the dervishes then turned their attention to Egypt. Only now was Aregawi able to get through to Metemma and send a letter to Flad telling him what had been happening to the Mission. C.M.J. agreed that Flad should prepare immediately to leave for Ethiopia, and when he arrived at Messawa in 1890 eight evangelists were there to greet him. During two weeks many misunderstandings were put straight and they were revived spiritually. He brought them a large supply of books and extra money to replace losses and to help the widows and orphans among the converts. The books included the newly revised Amharic Bible, Pilgrim's Progress, Isenberg's Church History, and others.

Famine and pestilence

The evangelists returned to a country groaning under famine due to the constant wars and occupations by soldiers. Typhus and cholera were widespread, and in that year alone many thousands died, including over a hundred and seventy Felasha converts. The greatest blow to the struggling Mission was the death of Debtera Biru only a month after the evangelists returned from Messawa. He was a wonderful soul winner, and had brought hundreds to faith in Christ. He was also used of God to build up the true converts in their faith, for his knowledge of the Bible was detailed and profound, and he was the Mission's living concordance. He was one of the few who treated the question of sin as seriously as it deserves, relied solely on God's grace and lived transparently.

After the death of the Emperor John, Minilik proclaimed himself Emperor but the local ruler of Begemdir resisted him and fighting continued. Plagues of locusts and caterpillars were added to the other miseries, and the wild animals increased in numbers and daring. One convert was killed in his own hut by a leopard. The money Flad had sent was soon

exhausted and more money was sent via the Swedish
missionaries at Adewa, but the messenger joined a caravan
leaving Adewa for Gonder which was attacked by robbers
who killed all of them. Food became scarce and cost ten
times as much, and some of the poorer people were reduced
to eating donkeys and hyenas.

In 1892 the dervishes attacked again, the country became
like a wilderness, and the Mission was heading for a crisis.
Aregawi, as leader, was missing Biru's wise counsel and
energy. Evangelistic tours were becoming more and more
difficult, and just continuing to live presented so many
problems that Aregawi asked if he could visit Flad in
Germany. There he explained how he had been compelled to
send the evangelists back to their weaving, and he himself had
lived on grass, roots and berries, because he had had no
training as a weaver. Flad thought that the Mission should be
ended, but C.M.J. admired the perseverance of the evangelists.
Eventually it was decided that Aregawi should return and
bring as many evangelists as possible to Messawa for one last
conference with Flad.

In February 1894 Flad started on his ninth and last journey
to Ethiopia and met five evangelists and four others. Aregawi
was made Field Leader and it was decided they would continue their present occupations, doing what they could in their
spare time until the province of Dembia was again populated.
There was a tearful parting because Flad was 63 and would
probably never see the evangelists again in Ethiopia.

Loneliness

In 1893 the Italians occupied the rest of Eritrea, but when
they tried to expand further the Emperor Minilik defeated
them at Adewa in 1896. The Italian attacks united all tribes
behind the Emperor, and the victory at Adewa led other
European powers to seek the friendship of Ethiopia, especially
after Minilik extended the southern borders as far as Kenya.
The French did most to connect Ethiopia with the outside
world by helping to create a system of posts and telephones,
and especially by building the railway to connect the
Emperor's new capital, Addis Abeba, with Jibouti on the
coast.

None of this helped to open up the country for the Mission, and loneliness proved more destructive than martyrdom. One or two Swedish missionaries were allowed to work in Addis Abeba, but a place as out of the way as Jenda was a different matter.

Aregawi obtained a permit to preach to the Felashas, and was tempted to take work in Addis Abeba, where one of those trained at St. Chrischona with him had become translator at the German Embassy, and later Mayor of the capital, but he realised that this would probably break the link with Flad and end the Mission. The link seemed small, consisting of faithful prayer and the exchange of letters, which continued after Flad had retired from his work in Europe in 1904.

A Jewish Counter Mission

By this time the evangelists were able to return to Jenda and to Azezo in Dembia, re-starting the schools and making some tours occasionally among the converts. They began to mention opposition through a gifted Jewish linguist named Jacob Faitlovitch, who obtained permission in 1904 to visit the Felashas. He estimated that they numbered then about 50,000. He was angered by the success of the Mission, and the following year appealed to all Jews to do something to oppose the work. He deplored that the Felashas had only thirty synagogues instead of over two hundred as in the past, though this was due much more to the Dervishes and famine than to the efforts of the Mission. Flad was greatly encouraged by this news. The spiritual results of the Mission must be real to be acknowledged in this way by such a man. He continued praying with more confidence.

The Jews of Europe sent Rabbi Nahum to check the reports of Faitlovitch, who had formed pro Felasha committees to help educate Felasha boys in Europe so that they could return and help win the tribe to modern Judaism. He was furious with Rabbi Nahum's report, published in 1908, which said that the Felashas were not Jews by blood, or very little so, that they were happier as they were, and that it was not worth while trying to teach them modern Judaism. He added that those Felashas who had become Christians had done so, not for money, as the Mission was very poor, but because they had accepted the Gospel. This was another unexpected and encouraging tribute.

In spite of the consequent opposition of the "Alliance Israelite" Faitlovitch started his own mission and made several journeys to the Felashas, but always avoided open discussion with the evangelists. He succeeded in preventing any more baptisms until 1909, by which time, of the 1,600 Felashas who had been baptised by the Mission, over 700 were still alive, scattered in many villages.

Cooling off

A year after their golden wedding in 1908 Mrs. Flad died and Martin Flad became practically blind. Their son, Frederick, had entered the ministry of the Church of England and was Head of the C.M.J. Mission in Tunis. He had taught himself some Amharic, so that on his frequent visits to his father he could help him with his Ethiopian correspondence until his father's death in 1915.

All contacts with the evangelists had been broken off in 1913 when the Emperor Minilik died. His grandson, Lij Iyasu, was a minor, and it was some time before a balance of power was achieved among the regents and advisers, by which time the Great War had started. As Lij Iyasu grew up and took more power into his own hands he was misled even more than Theodore had been by a false prophecy that a new Mahdi would arise from an unexpected quarter and rule all Moslems in East Africa. Lij Iyasu, whose father had been a Moslem until forced to become a Christian by King John, now became a Moslem.

Ras Teferi was the son of the Emperor Menelik's late cousin and favourite general. In 1916 the Christian nobles, after being absolved by the Abuna, rebelled against Lij Iyasu under Ras Teferi's leadership, and put Minilik's daughter Zewditu on the throne. Ras Teferi became Regent and Heir Apparent.

During this time the difficulties of the evangelists increased, and with no help possible from Europe they became discouraged. It was evident that the work had not become sufficiently indigenous, and there were doubts whether the Mission could survive. All converts had been baptised into the Orthodox Church, which did not have sufficient life either to make a spiritual home for them nor to encourage the evangelists in their work.

New Hope

After the Great War, Frederick Flad heard that the Regent, Ras Teferi, had asked for foreign help of all kinds, including missionaries, and that the Swedes had been able to restart their work in Addis Abeba and Adewa. He applied to return, but permits and arrangements for the journey took so long that he did not arrive at Addis Abeba until 1922. Owing to the illness of a messenger no evangelists were there to meet him, but the Mayor was very helpful in obtaining interviews with the Regent, who thanked him for all Martin Flad had done and readily gave the permits to visit Jenda.

Frederick Flad said he thought he had learnt patience in Tunis but when he got to Ethiopia he found he had none. After three months four evangelists arrived and he set off for Jenda. There he was given a full account of all that was being done and saw the ruins of the old mission station. Aregawi was delighted to see the son of the man he loved and respected so much, and he estimated that of nearly 2,000 Felashas who had been baptised about 500 were still living. Aregawi, although 75 years old, was determined to accompany Flad on his return journey to Asmara. On the way the caravan leader was suddenly seized and chained to a man to whom he owed money, as was the custom. Flad, in order to avoid a probable long delay, paid the money himself and was given a receipt duly authenticated by the thumb prints of the witnesses.

At Asmara a Swedish missionary asked him to revise a manuscript of the New Testament translated into Amharic by Ethiopians. Aregawi was the obvious one to do this and Flad persuaded him to go with him to Europe. They reached St. Chrischona in 1923 in time to attend the 50th anniversary of Aregawi's dedication there as an evangelist to his own people. He so inspired the students as to the need to renew the Mission that six of them volunteered. C.M.J. had very little money, but extra gifts made it possible for two of them, Heintze and Baur, to do some extra training before going to Ethiopia. Aregawi stayed long enough to help revise the New Testament in Amharic, which was printed at the royal press in Addis Abeba after he returned to Jenda.

9

HOPE BROADENED AGAIN

A New Start

WHEN HEINTZE and Baur reached Addis Abeba in 1926 there
were no missionaries in what was then known as British,
French and Italian Somaliland, Northern Kenya and Eastern
Sudan, and very few in Eritrea and Ethiopia. Permits for the
interior were not easy to obtain, and the Regent, Ras Teferi,
was the only important man in the Government to favour
missionaries. His position was made less secure, especially
by the Church, when he introduced some foreign customs and
opened the first modern school in Addis Abeba in 1926, but
the very conservative Abuna died later that year as did Ras
Teferi's rival for power under the Empress. He then called
in the war lords to acknowledge his supremacy. Dejjazmach
Bolcha of Sidamo refused to come until 1927, when he
arrived with an "escort" of 10,000 men. Ras Teferi invited
him to a great feast, which he agreed to attend only if he could
"honour Ras Teferi with a guard of 600 men". While the
feasting was prolonged Ras Teferi's soldiers were at work
amongst the ruler of Sidamo's 10,000 escort camped on the
edge of Addis Abeba. Most were persuaded to agree to sell
their arms and go home, and the few who refused were
scourged. Dejjazmach Bolcha returned at night to find only
the ashes of many fires, and eventually took refuge in a
church. So Ras Teferi forgave him on condition that he
became a monk!

In 1928 Ras Teferi's supremacy as Heir Apparent was
recognised by his being crowned king, so when the Empress
Zewditu died in 1930 he was crowned Emperor, King of
Kings, and took the throne name Haile Selassie, which means
"The Power of the Trinity."

In 1927 Ras Teferi had eventually granted Heintze and
Baur a permit to go to Jenda. The 300 mile journey by mule
normally took six weeks, but there were delays on the way
and Heintze and Baur did not arrive until just before the
rainy season started, so they had to live in tents during the

heavy rains, postponing any building until the three months' rainy season had ended. The nearest doctor or mission station was three weeks' journey away. There were no roads, or carts, or shops, so whatever they needed, which they had not been able to bring on the back of a mule, they had to make. Large trees, needed for making planks for doors or furniture were scarce, and these were cut up by digging pits in the ground and using a two-handed saw with one man in the pit and another above. While the work of building was going on the remaining evangelists were set to work teaching the children and going on preaching tours, but after such a long gap they did not take kindly to supervision, and some of them had become lazy. For their own safety the missionaries were given guards and ordered not to go too far from Jenda, but Heintze slipped away and toured the countryside to find out where the Felashas were living.

In 1928 when the Emperor was still Regent he had asked Frederick Flad to educate his daughter as Switzerland is a neutral country. Frederick Flad's daughter, Lola, offered to be Princess Tsehai's governess, and the Princess, then ten years old, lived with the Flad family for two years near Vevey. In 1930 Lola took the Princess back to Ethiopia for three months. During that time Heintze and Lola became engaged and were married the following year in Switzerland. When they returned to Jenda with two single missionaries they found Aregawi was dying but well enough to sing one more hymn of praise with them.

During Heintze's absence Baur spent the year treating patients in the mornings and teaching in the afternoons. His only contact with the outside world was a monthly messenger with his mail from Metemma on the Sudanese border. These messengers had to walk through hot lowlands where there were more wild animals than people. At night they would climb up into a tree and tie themselves in a sort of wooden bower to branches so that they would not fall down when asleep. Baur was a gentle and humble man of considerable ability who had given up a promising business career to become a missionary. He spoke several languages, had mastered Amharic well, and had gained the affection of the ordinary country Ethiopians. Heintze, on the other hand,

believed the Gospel could be spread more effectively through
the priests, nobles, and more educated Ethiopians. For this
and other reasons the two men decided to separate, Baur
being drawn to another tribe called the K'imants. Before
starting on this new field Baur went home for a short furlough
of three months, during which time he became engaged to
another of Frederick Flad's daughters. To avoid a year's delay
in putting up buildings he returned when the thatching grass
was ready to be cut.

An extension to the K'imants

On his return journey Baur had to take the more dangerous
and exacting alternative route because the Blue Nile was in
full flood, but he had the compensation of passing through
Mek'dela and Lalibela, and must have been one of the first
Europeans to see the scene of the famous battle of sixty years
before. The churches of Lalibela are the only ones in the
world which are complete buildings hewn out of the solid
rock.

The K'imants are not scattered like the Felashas but occupy
an area west of Gonder. Many lived in or near their chief
town of Ch'ilga, so Baur built his new station there. Most
of this tribe of about 80,000 had been forced to become
nominal Christians by the Emperors Theodore and John.
They are one of the Agau tribes who are mainly farmers
owning their own land. They were rather lax in their
family life and were despised by the Amharas as "hewers
of wood and drawers of water." Their original religion
was a strange mixture of Jewish and pagan. For example,
they believed in only one Supreme God, who is an unseen
Spirit, but they worship angels and their ancestors as
mediators, and know little about their religion for they
have no sacred books. They offer sacrifices, but these have
nothing to do with sin, they are vows or bargains made
with God for rain and such like. They observe the laws of
purification and the Mosaic distinctions between clean and
unclean meats, and practice circumcision, but will not eat
with the Felashas. Saturdays are their days of rest but not
necessarily of worship, which is conducted on wooded hill
tops. They have a system of confession to priests, but rely

on the Feast of Remembrance after death to free them from sin and save them from Hell.

C.M.J. called them "half Jews" and was glad to see this extension, but in April 1932, only a few weeks after starting to build the new station, Baur was taken ill with fever and dysentry, and sent for Heintze. Two days after he arrived Baur died, commending Heintze to God's care.

It was about this time that three of the Mission huts were burnt by lightning, and the Mission was transferred to the old site where Martin Flad had been, though by then it had become rather isolated. The following year the two missionaries who had gone to Ethiopia with Heintze after his previous furlough returned to Switzerland and were replaced by four others, including Sister Lina Lerner. When one missionary got ill he was isolated and a bell was fixed in her hut with a long string to his bed. She had just gone to bed when there was a loud ringing of this bell. She got up and was about to go to him when the night watchman came to tell her not to worry, a bull had blundered into the string.

In 1934 Heintze was able to arrange a two-day conference attended by 200 Felashas of whom all but 30 were former converts. Also present was a former Moslem teacher, who had been led by the references to Jesus in the Koran to study the New Testament through which he was converted to Christ. This was similar to the experience of his leader, Sheik Zachariah in 1910, through whose witness about 4,000 Moslems had been converted and joined the Ethiopian Church. Unfortunately, the Adventists came later and persuaded many to join them and oppose the Church. After the conference at Jenda this former Moslem teacher helped the evangelists to take the Gospel to the Moslems as well as the Felashas.

Hopes deferred again

In 1934 Heintze took his wife to Switzerland for the birth of their son, and then returned to Ethiopia with two young men. Convinced that the Italians would soon invade Ethiopia he had left his wife in Switzerland. After a few months he returned home with three of the missionaries who were in a poor state of health.

In October 1935 the Italians invaded the country and the
Ethiopians, as usual, fought bravely and well, but rifles and
spears were no match for aeroplanes, tanks and poison gas.
After seven months the Italians marched into Addis Abeba
and the Emperor escaped by rail to Jibouti. Two months
earlier the Italians had captured Gonder and because of the
previous advice of the Italian Consul, the three young men
who had been left behind at Jenda left the country through
the Sudan. The help, especially medical, which they had given
the Ethiopian troops was too well known. Heintze's favourite
evangelist, Alek'a Fett'ena, was left in charge. For four
years the Italians left him in peace allowing him to hold
services and meetings in the church, which was not completed
until after they arrived, and they even forwarded to him
the money Heintze sent.

What spiritual fruit had the ten years work produced? For
various reasons there was little to see. No missionary except
Heintze had stayed much longer than it takes to learn the
difficult language of Amharic, and he was much occupied
with building, exploring and training. Baur's death increased
his fear of disease and prevented a closer contact with those
they had sought to win. Of his zeal there was no doubt. He
and Baur once fasted completely from all food for nearly three
weeks to pray the more earnestly for conversions. Also some
of the older evangelists were often a handicap. Some of them
kept slaves secretly and resisted all attempts to be shown
that this was wrong. They also put such an emphasis on Giiz
that they were inclined to think the Gospel must always be
preached first in this ancient, but dead, language. They wasted
much time teaching Giiz to the boys, and accepted the common opinion that educating girls was unnecessary. Only his
indomitable will enabled Heintze to continue in the face of
these and other difficulties and in such isolation. In 1936 he
began to learn Italian and went to Italy more than once
seeking permission to return to Ethiopia, but it was not to be.

A more direct approach

When the Mission was founded Gonder was virtually the
capital of Ethiopia, but by 1935 Addis Abeba had for long

occupied that position. The Emperor's palace was there, and the Abuna and the Chief Monk also lived there. If new life was to be brought to the Ethiopian Church this was now the better place to make an approach.

Alfred Buxton had helped to start the World-wide Evangelisation Crusade in the Congo with his father-in-law C. T. Studd, and after that, with Dr. Lambie, he founded the Abyssinia Frontiers Mission, which was later merged with the Sudan Interior Mission. He then started a new work in Northern Kenya under the Bible Churchmen's Missionary Society. Three years later, in 1931, he was still anxious to take the Gospel into unevangelised fields. Not daring to tell B.C.M.S. of his longing, he went in faith with no financial backing northwards into Ethiopia itself by an unknown route of 700 miles. He had previously met Frederick Flad and heard of the effort to bring new life to the Ethiopian Church through converted Felashas. After reaching Addis Abeba he became convinced that a direct approach to the Church would be the key to the evangelisation of the whole of Ethiopia. To his great joy B.C.M.S. was now willing to support him in this. Martin Flad's translation was known as the foreign or Protestant Bible, and Buxton's first thought was that a translation by Ethiopians would be more acceptable and effective.

Towards the end of 1934 he brought from England to Addis Abeba his wife and six young men to start a Bible School in a house rented near the market place instead of in the European quarter with the other missions. One missionary originally sent out by C.M.J. was also taken on by Buxton at this time. The first four Ethiopians to join them gave up good salaries to enter this Bible School and learned to live by faith. Soon they began to preach at the Cathedral until the priests eventually forbade them to do so.

When the Italians declared war on Ethiopia in 1935 the official attitude of the Church changed, and they were encouraged to preach to the troops and to the crowds on national occasions. Buxton kept himself in the background. He found that parts of the manuscript of Blatten Geyta Hiruy revised by Frederick Flad had been printed as separate Gospels, which he distributed enthusiastically amongst the troops, for he felt that they were more acceptable to the Ethiopians than the older translations.

In 1937 Marshal Graziani, the Viceroy, was wounded by bombs while distributing gifts among the poor on a feast day. Once again we see how the use of force spoils the work of God. Large numbers of Ethiopians, especially of the more educated ones, were massacred as a reprisal, and several leaders of the Ethiopian Church were martyred, including some of Buxton's preachers who had risen to 12 in number. After that all missionaries were ordered to leave the country.

10

ANOTHER BEGINNING

BEFORE THE Emperor Haile Selassie left Ethiopia in 1936 he sent special messages to the Christians in England asking them to pray for his country. He admitted to one missionary that he had put too much trust in the League of Nations and politics and too little trust in God. On 5th May 1941, exactly five years after the Italians occupied Addis Abeba, the Emperor re-entered it from the Sudan with the help of British troops, and one of his first proclamations was to re-open his country to missionaries.

Buxton's vision taken up again

David Stokes was one of the six men who accompanied Alfred Buxton in 1934, and he was one of the first to take advantage of the Emperor's proclamation. When war was declared he was working among Ethiopian refugees in Kenya. He joined the British Army in the Sudan and was transferred later to Addis Abeba. He got there by a taxi commandeered in Khartoum, which had neither spare tyres nor tools! In 1942 he was able to re-start the B.C.M.S. Bible School, the aim of which was to send Orthodox Christians back to their own Church to preach the Word there and become the means of new life. But after some years they found that instead of this almost all of them were being employed by other Missions, most of which were establishing their own churches, some even being opposed to the Orthodox Church. Also as young men soon found that they could rise much higher educationally and socially by entering government schools the number of students had been falling off, so in 1955 the men's department was closed, but the women's department, which had been started later and was not affected in the same way, was continued. B.C.M.S. then concentrated on literature, and David Stokes, who had already written some comment-aries, became a leading member of the Committee of Ethiopians and Europeans commissioned by the Emperor to re-translate the Amharic Bible. Alfred Buxton had been killed during the bombing of London, and gifts made in his memory were used to distribute copies of this new translation among the priests and monks of the Ethiopian Church. The whole population is now accepting it, because the Emperor and the bishops have authorised it.

Knowing what the Authorised Version of the Bible did to revive the Church of England in the 16th century when translated into the language of the people, we thank God for what C.M.J., B.C.M.S. and the Bible Society have done to provide the people of Ethiopia with many thousands of copies of the Bible in Amharic.

Another Englishman sent to Ethiopia

C.M.J. was anxious to re-start the work in Ethiopia, preferably by an Englishman, and there was much prayer that the right man be found. I entered the ministry of the Church of England in 1942 and was appointed to a curacy in Bath, the city where the Emperor spent most of his exile. On a visit to my parish in 1944 the General Secretary of C.M.J. said he was looking for some one to re-start the Mission to the Felashas in Ethiopia. I wondered if this was a call from God to me. As an undergraduate at Cambridge I had heard God's call to the mission field, and wondered whether He wanted me to go to central Africa, or whether he wanted me to follow my uncles and aunts who had done their missionary service in Nigeria, but no door to these countries had opened. I remembered seeing a C.M.J. "Palestine Exhibition" some years before, which not only made the Bible come to life but showed clearly the need to take the Gospel to the Jews. The more I learned about the work that had been done among the Felashas the more this door seemed to open, and so God led me to offer to go to Ethiopia.

After C.M.J. accepted me I did a few months training at the Missionary School of Medicine and was ready to leave, but with the war just ending it was well nigh impossible for a civilian to get a passage on a boat, or a visa to Ethiopia. However, Bishop Gwynn, who knew my family in Egypt, had an idea. He suggested I took a commission as an Army Chaplain if he could persuade the Chaplain General to post me to the British Military Mission in Ethiopia. I joined the army and reached Addis Abeba in January 1946.

In the Army

The British Military Mission was scattered throughout Ethiopia, so my duties as Chaplain took me to almost every province and gave me a good idea of the country as a whole. On one of these trips I reached Lake T'ana, procured mules and an interpreter, and went on to Jenda, hoping to find Alek'a Fett'ena, the former chief evangelist, looking after the mission. Instead we found none of the evangelists and the whole place in ruins.

After being left in peace for four years Fett'ena's activities had been interrupted when the Mission buildings were occupied by Eritrean troops, and in the ensuing fighting in 1940 the Church was burnt. Fett'ena went to Gonder to get a permit to start a school, and in his absence people living near Jenda had stripped the Mission buildings of furniture, doors, windows and roofs. They had then threatened him if he complained to the authorities. Fett'ena had lost his wife the year before and had been imprisoned by both sides in turn, so understandably had become discouraged. There had not been enough money to pay any of the evangelists, so they had found secular employment, and after a while he did the same, finding work in another place.

The local people were keen on the school being re-started, but did not seem to be interested in the spiritual side, which I took as a sign that I should seek elsewhere for a mission site.

During the war a group called "the Friends of Ethiopia" had been formed to pray specially for the Felashas. I wrote to them regularly and stressed the need for recruits, but the only ones to respond were my mother and sister, who went out in 1947 and became matron and nurse at Gonder Hospital for a year. During this year I was demobilised and could re-start the Mission. Ato Kebbeda, an Amhara deacon from the province of Begemdir, had attended the B.C.M.S. Bible School, where he had been amazed to hear that salvation is not by good works but by faith in Christ. When he and his wife heard that we were going to re-start a mission in his own province he asked if he might join us. Here was another man of humble origin who proved to be definitely chosen of God.

Building up a new work

Before going to Ethiopia I had pictured myself going from
one group of Felasha huts to another while living in a tent,
but it soon became clear that I would have to establish some
centre from which to work. I was led to choose a place two
miles from the town of Dabat which was 8,650 feet high,
80 miles north of Jenda and had a population of under
5,000. It was on the only road in that part of the country, one
which connected Gonder with Asmera. We chose a compound
on a brow of a small hill with four small Italian-built houses
designed as a farm, but it was more than six months before
the contract was signed. It gave us about 14 acres of land
for thirty years at a reasonable rent. The houses needed doors,
windows, and repairs to the roofs, and everything scraped
clean and re-plastered, for the local people had illegally
occupied the buildings with their cattle. Each family had done
their cooking from an open fire on the floor of every room,
just as they did in their own huts, which of course have no
chimneys. With no public transport, everything we needed
had to be brought by means of the occasional passing trader's
lorry. Not being a sterling area no money could be sent from
Britain for capital expenditure, so we had to do everything
ourselves and as cheaply as possible, and I was grateful
to friends who sent me books about building.

The local Amhara people had been turned out by the
Government, but they tried a number of times to plough the
land rented to us, so our first priority was to build a mile
long wall of loose stones. Some of the friendship we lost over
this we regained by enlisting their help in getting materials and
putting the buildings in order. The nearest European was 50
miles away and Kebbeda was the only man on whom I could
rely, so I was forced to learn Amharic and the customs of the
country by jumping in alone at the deep end. Digging a well
60 feet deep was another problem, because demons were
thought to dwell in the regions below 30 feet. As we were so
far from civilisation we had to become as self sufficient as
possible in everything, including milk, because if the local
people sold milk to foreigners they were sure their cows would
die. Some had started to sell it to Arab traders living in Dabat,
two miles away, and their cows had died, which proved it!

So the Mission had to have its own cows as well as bulls to plough the land, donkeys to carry corn from the market, sheep to provide meat, and horses and mules for trekking. We had to plant eucalyptus trees for fuel and future building, and lay out a kitchen garden and the beginnings of an orchard.

After a few months, although windows had not been fitted in the houses, my mother and sister joined me. A clinic was started, and gradually the Felashas from the nearby villages began to come for treatment. Later, through Frederick Flad, a Chrischona trained plumber and his wife offered to join us as missionaries, and arrived in 1950 with a lorry load of materials which we bought in Asmera, for now we were building several huts. He arrived in time to put the piping in from the well and install the hand pump. I began to make exploratory trips and gave Bibles to some Felashas and Christian priests and monks. At Dabat I started classes and spent much time instructing the two evangelists, Kebbeda and Teshoma.

It was more than five years since I had left England. Furlough was overdue, and it was clear that the prayer letters were not going to produce the recruits needed for such a large area, but we were encouraged by being able to open the new clinic, and David Stokes of B.C.M.S. happened to be visiting Gonder and came to dedicate it. He prophesied that the walls would crack in two years and fall down in five. Fortunately he proved to be a good friend but a bad prophet.

Two days before I left Dabat two letters arrived, one from C.M.J. saying there was no money for recruits, and the other from Switzerland saying that Frederick Flad had died at the age of 87. Before he died he had arranged a month's deputation work for me in Switzerland. Although bands of armed robbers had stopped all trains between Eritrea and the Sudan I was sure the Lord would see me through, and I found a truck driver who was willing to risk the journey to the Eritrean border. There the local Chief of Police gave me no hope of going on, but seeing my determination he gave me his own jeep and driver which the border guards in both countries recognised and so waved us through. After Ethiopian mules and lorries I found the taxi drive in Cairo to the C.M.J. English Mission College quite terrifying. The driver was furious at finding certain streets blocked by the cavalcade of King Farouk. After a short rest I went to buy my boat ticket and found I had been given the wrong travellers cheques, but the Lord had provided. I had in my wallet a cheque for American dollars, enough to pay my third class fare to Switzerland to arrive just in time for my engagements there.

11

MARRIAGE AND ALLIANCES

St. Chrischona joins in again

WHEN I REACHED Switzerland I was thrilled to find that Mrs. Flad and her five daughters had such a deep concern for the work of the Mission that they had clearly been giving much prayer support. After a few days' rest I left for a two weeks' speaking tour to Swiss towns, including, of course, St. Chrischona, which had provided so many missionaries in the past. There had been difficulties under my predecessor over leadership and St. Chrischona wanted more direct control over their own workers. C.M.J. agreed to this, but it did not prevent further differences arising.

After my visits to St. Chrischona and Beatenberg Bible School six recruits offered for Ethiopia. One of these was Sister Lina Lerner, a nurse who had served at Jenda and offered to go back, and the others were another nurse, a teacher and a married couple. All were accepted, and this decision was confirmed when, during my furlough, though a number of others in England were interested, not one offered for service in Ethiopia.

Marriage

As a missionaries' child I had had very little home life and was much attracted by the family life of the Flads. Two daughters were unmarried and I soon fell in love with the younger one, Christine. The Lord knew I would not propose to her unless she was called by Him to the work in Ethiopia. Before I left for the two weeks speaking tour Christine told me she believed God was calling her to work among the Felashas. How quickly the Lord works sometimes! We both prayed about it for the two weeks, and when I returned we became engaged. Christine was a nurse and Bible trained, but had stayed at home to nurse her father. He had requested that an appeal be made at his funeral for the mission field, and to her surprise Christine felt that she herself was the one being called by God through this appeal. Four weeks later I arrived.

We were married in July 1951, and I took with me on our honeymoon a letter from K'es Asris which had just arrived. As a boy he had attended a school started by Dr. Faitlovitch, and was so gifted that Dr. Faitlovitch wanted to send him to Europe to be educated. His parents would not let him go but sent him to Felasha monks for training to become a priest. During my first months at Dabat Asris heard that an Englishman had come to help the Felashas, which to him was incredible because he thought Christians always persecuted Jews. A nearby funeral gave him the opportunity to try to find out the real reason for my coming. To his surprise he was pointed to his own Jewish prophets and what they said about the coming of the Messiah. Later his wife's health gave him added excuses for coming, without which his fellow Jews would have got suspicious, and each time he was shown more about the Messiah and given literature. He finally started reading the New Testament, and became convinced shortly before I left for furlough that Jesus was his Saviour and Messiah. The Adventists, who had started a mission several years before at Debra Tabor, heard of this and persuaded him to go to them for baptism. After setting out on the long journey he wondered if an injury to his knee and also a dream he had were signs that he should go back, and he was relieved later to find the Adventist missionary had been called away. The letter gave the assurance of his faith in Christ and desire for baptism. The Lord could hardly have given to us a better wedding present.

When we reached Dabat we received a great welcome, but my mother could not join in because she was seriously ill with typhus, having previously had pneumonia twice. Now nearing her seventieth birthday she had bravely faced hardships like a young pioneer for years, but it was clearly time for her to go home to a more comfortable life. My sister was due for furlough and was able to take our mother back with her to England.

The work develops

I went on several long treks visiting the widely scattered Felashas and finding out what kind of life they led. On one such trip I went with Asris and Kebbeda towards the Sudan border. Our guardian angels were hard at work as we were going along a valley followed by armed robbers who were interested in the boxes we were carrying. Though told by the villagers that the boxes contained only books and medicines the robbers came up to us when we were bathing at a river. When asked if we had guards I pointed to the sky and said "God is a better guard than many soldiers". They went away, but two or three days later in the very same spot they attacked police taking taxes to Dabat, killing two of the police and taking all the money. On another trip to the Simeyn mountains we saw Felasha monks sacrifice the Passover lamb and sprinkle its blood round the synagogue door. In a public debate the next day the monks refused to be impressed by the prophecies concerning Jesus Christ, and said they believed only the writings of Moses.

I had started Men's classes as soon as I returned from furlough, which later grew to an average attendance of about twenty. At first the classes were for two weeks but later I was able to arrange longer ones. Those who attended a full week were given a Bible.

Asris was very keen to learn. He had realised that his witch-doctoring was sinful, even though he had practised it only on Gentiles, and when former customers kept calling for charms or to have their fortunes told, he had gone to live in another village. He had been thrilled at the prospect of being baptised with his family by the priests of the Ethiopian Church as it would mean unity with the Amharas instead of joining some foreign minority church. Later he developed a more mature love which made him want to help towards the renewal of the Ethiopian Church.

In 1953 three more families were baptized, including that of Ato Mekketa, whose father had been a witch doctor and later became a nominal Christian. To Mekketa the most important part of his religion was a regular observance of the Sabbath, which he believed atoned for all his sins, including that of leaving his wife occasionally for other women. Like many Felashas he believed that the worst sin a Jew can commit is to become a Christian. However, reading a tract at the clinic led him to attend some of the classes, and later after living in the compound for a year, his wife was convinced

that he had entered a new life and that his new faith was the
true one, and so the whole family was baptised.

The Swiss teacher and Sister Lina had arrived in 1952, the
German couple in 1953 and the German nurse in 1955. A
small day and boarding school had gradually grown until by
1955 there were fifty boarders. New huts and houses were
constantly being built until we had a small village of about
40 buildings.

Unexpected difficulties

An old landrover had been bought with gifts from Mission
friends of the Flad family. Our first child Elizabeth was born
in Addis Abeba in 1953 and when she was nearly a year old
she and her mother fell out of the landrover when a door
gave way on a hairpin bend. Christine was not too badly hurt
but a child specialist at Asmera later said that Elizabeth's
brain would be permanently affected, and this was confirmed
by Swiss doctors when Christine took Elizabeth to Switzerland. My wife also had to have two major operations and it
was a year before she was able to return to Ethiopia.

Another disappointment had been an unexpected government order in 1952 which prohibited all preaching and teaching by missionaries outside Mission compounds. We all
prayed very much that God would reverse this, and had high
hopes when Christine and I were granted an audience with
the Emperor. But gradually it became clear that God's answer
was No. As we were no longer allowed to go to the Felashas
we had to think of ways to get them to come to us. This
meant concentrating the more on training Ethiopians to go
out and do what we missionaries were not allowed to do. We
arranged that the men's classes were to be for longer periods,
and began making preparations for turning the classes into a
residential Families Bible School, which later proved to be
the part of the work which God blessed most.

There followed difficulties with staff. After two years with
the Mission the Swiss missionary plumber gave us a shock
when he said he had come to believe that the baptism of
infants was wrong and he would resign after six months. We
could not but agree with the practice of the Ethiopian Church
in baptizing children of all ages with their parents, and saw

the blessing which came from so avoiding splits within families. Yet, unfortunately, the German couple left two years later for a similar reason.

There was trouble, too, with the Seventh Day Adventists at Debra Tabor. Having more money for buildings, books and equipment than we had, they were able to attract some of our adults and children, but God heard our prayers and virtually all of these rejected their teaching in the end. Then came difficulties with the Jehovah's Witnesses who tried to infiltrate our Families' School, and like the Adventists were able to offer higher salaries to graduates. But the work of their Mission was badly damaged when they employed Teshoma, who had been dismissed by us as an evangelist because we found that he had a predilection for stealing and for women. When the Jehovah's Witnesses found this out for themselves, and also dismissed him, he committed suicide.. Prayer was again answered when so many complaints about the Jehovah's Witnesses were made by other Missions, and also by the Orthodox Church, that the government stopped all their activities in Ethiopia.

The Jewish Counter Mission was a much more serious challenge to our work. With support from the Israeli Government it had quickly developed its activities among the Felashas, and established 35 schools in the province of Begemdir, a boarding school in Asmera, and a school in Jerusalem to which they sent by air the more promising children. This led us to pray the more, and led the Israeli Government to consider the possibility of helping the Felashas to go to Israel. But were the Felashas really Jews, and could they be integrated successfully into the life in Israel? These doubts finally prevailed and Israel stopped sending any more grants. By 1958 there were only a few village schools left, supported by gifts from American Jews.

Compensations

In our struggles with Adventists, Jehovah's Witnesses, and the Counter Mission, the instruction given at the Men's Classes was of great value. When approached by these and other people they were able to give reasons for their new found faith based on the Bible. After I returned from furlough in 1955 we were able to restart the Bible School as a residential Families School with husbands and wives learning together. The patient work of Sister Lina Lerner for several months among the women living on the compound had convinced some of them that they could learn just as well as the men. None of the families were able to afford to stay for the whole length of the course, so the Mission provided them with accommodation and enough money for food and clothes only. It was mainly the attraction of education which caused them to risk the disruption consequent upon leaving their homes and rented farms for two or three years. The aim of the School was that each family which had been converted to Christ during the first year should stay on for a second year and then return to their village and take up their previous employment, witnessing to others for love of Christ and without payment from the Mission.

While teaching in the Families' School I concentrated on the training of two of the first converts, Asris and Mekketa, together with my old friend Kebbeda. First we showed Mekketa how to teach the 250 odd characters of the Amharic alphabet to the first class, which did not know how to read and write. Then Kebbeda took over the second class and Asris the third, the one for committed Christians. By the time I was due for furlough again in 1959 they were able to do all the teaching alone.

I was keen that the work should be indigenous as much as possible, and not dependent on Mission money, especially in the villages. The Felashas are a country tribe, who consider that any one of them who goes to live in a town has broken his faith. I had found from experience and from other Missions that any child trained beyond fourth grade in an elementary school was unwilling to go back to the country, and so would automatically leave his tribe if he was a Felasha Jew. For this reason the children's section of the Families' School was only to the fourth grade, and for the same reason all buildings were in simple country style, with food, clothes and all amenities to match. But the leader of the St. Chrischona missionaries was the Swiss teacher, whose heart naturally rebelled against the acceptance of any sort of ceiling, whether to equipment or education.

Differences among the Missionaries

The seven Missionaries from Switzerland and Germany belonged to pietist groups working within the Lutheran Church. It was not surprising that after a while these missionaries found it irksome to conform to a policy laid down by the Mission of the Church of England. They became more and more unhappy about converts being baptised by priests of the Ethiopian Church, they wanted better and not native style school buildings, and would like higher classes, formed in the schools, so that the children could go on to further education, instead of educating them only sufficiently to return to their villages to make an effective witness there with their parents. After a number of joint committee meetings in London and Switzerland it was decided to give the Swiss and Germans the station at Jenda under their own committees, while we remained at Dabat with the Families' School and a clinic. There was a larger clinic at Jenda, and a small elementary school.

The Swiss teacher began to build at Jenda in 1958 with a view to transferring the children's boarding school to there. His aim was eventually to place teachers in as many Felasha villages as possible paid by St. Chrischona.

When the authorities realised that he was dealing with them about Jenda instead of me, they began to suspect that this was a back-door method of introducing a new Mission into Ethiopia, and withdrew their permit to build there. This was just before I went home on furlough in 1959, leaving the Families School in the hands of the Ethiopian evangelists.

It is perhaps not surprising that there had been fewer baptisms of Felashas during the past four years, but in the mercy of God there had been some.

A remarkable conversion

Bishat was a Felasha woman who had borne her husband 14 children, most of whom had died. Her mother was a witch doctor, and when she died her "zar" was said to have possessed Bishat. When her husband saw that Bishat was now possessed he left her. Like most of these witchdoctors, she was not in good health and came to the clinic in 1954. She was allowed to stay on the compound for six months, but rarely came to prayers and tried to continue her witch-doctoring. When her nephew, Ato Mekketa, convinced her that this could not be allowed, she went to Simeyn for two years, where such practices are very common. Here she became known as a powerful witchdoctor. She described how her "zar" would speak to her in dreams when clients came to be healed, telling her to get them to eat certain meat or roots, or milk etc. She claimed that most of those who obeyed her were healed.

Her brother brought her back to the Mission in 1957, where many prayed for her. Nearly a year later God spoke to her through a dream (as is not uncommon with Africans) in which she saw a black king come to the compound with hundreds of soldiers. Her "zar" was with him and told her to drink from her mother's cup, or sit on her mother's stool. She refused to do either and four soldiers seized her. Then Ato Kebbeda came with a sword to deliver her and all fled. Kebbeda then gave her a dove which she received. She discussed the dream with Kebbeda and his wife, and came to believe that it was an invitation to receive the Spirit of Christ, which she did. The "zar" never came upon her again.

Two months later Bishat was baptised with her smaller children, and continued at the Bible School. During one holiday she went to Mach'a near Wuzava, which has the biggest concentration of Felasha villages in Ethiopia. Here friends and relatives planned to get her "zar" to possess her again. They brought her into a hut where there were three witch-doctors, who started their incantations and clapping. When she got over her surprise she stood up and sang a hymn in honour of Christ. One by one those three witchdoctors left the hut, and she continued to witness to the people who remained.

12

WHAT WILL HAPPEN?

Building up again

We went on furlough in 1959, and were thankful for a solution to one problem, in that God provided a school in England for Elizabeth after we had come to the end of our possibilities, and then He added in His goodness a Christian Trust which paid the fees.

Meanwhile, the Swiss and German missionaries sent in their resignations, and then we did the same to give C.M.J. a free hand in choosing between the two policies. They decided unanimously to send us back, and although we still tried to find a compromise this proved impossible. Six of them joined other Missions and Sister Lina stayed with us.

However, this break came at the right time, for I had just completed the training of the Ethiopian evangelist-teachers, who continued teaching the Families' School in Dabat, while Christine ran the clinic there and Sister Lina the one at Jenda. Both clinics grew in numbers and won many friends for the Mission. I concentrated for a time on the Children's Schools at both stations 80 miles apart. There were problems in plenty, for the only source of teachers we could draw on were our own older children in the schools, aged about 15, and also there was only one indifferent mechanic at Gonder between both stations.

Yet another problem started during our furlough in 1959, when the local Member of Parliament had accused the Mission of having more land than the Government had allowed in the contract, and claimed that the alleged excess land was his own. The trouble arose through a government official's use of ropes and the forearm of a tall man to measure the area. The matter was heard in successive courts, and, to our great joy, the Swiss teacher, who had been praying about reconciliation with us, took on much of the responsibility for the tiring business with the courts when the case reached Addis Abeba.

Eventually, in 1966, when Mr. Heintze's son Wilfred was visiting us in Ethiopia, he went to see Ras Imeru, the premier noble of Ethiopia, whom he had got to know in Switzerland. With Ras Imeru's help the Dabat land case was finally settled out of court, with generous financial help from him and other friends. A similar law case had arisen over the Jenda land, which was solved much more easily when Wilfred suddenly discovered a map of the boundaries among his father's papers, and sent it on the off chance that it might be of interest to me! To many Ethiopians court cases are the most enjoyable national sport, but when both these matters had been cleared up we felt profoundly thankful to God.

The Families' School

As the Felashas were so poor it was impossible to have a residential Families' School without the Mission supporting all students with just enough for food and clothes, but we were always very wary about creating "rice Christians", or employing men who came primarily for the money. For this reason the wages of the evangelists and teachers also were kept down to a level below that of other missions and of course still further below that of the Government. Also, to help with integration, the Ethiopian staff was purposely of different tribes.

K'es Ferreda was an Amhara country priest of the Orthodox Church of Birra. He had been content with the typical beliefs of his area, that salvation is by fasting and other "good works," provided a man appeals to Mary and other mediators between God and men. But he began to question this seriously when I went to Birra in a tent for three weeks in the early days. Some time later he was one of the first priests to come to the Men's Classes, where he turned fully to Christ. Only after that did he come of himself through the Bible to the truth that Jesus is the only Mediator between God and men.[1] Nobody had preached against Mary or the saints to him, we had merely preached Christ. From 1959 to 1960 he came with his wife to the Families' School, and was made a trial evangelist in 1961, eventually becoming a full evangelist

(i) 1 Tim. 2.5.

at Jenda. In 1972 he took the place of Asris as the leading teacher of the Families' School at Dabat, after Asris had been ordained a priest of the Ethiopian Orthodox church and retired.

The employment of these men was to take advantage of another answer to prayer and patient waiting. I had had to go to Addis Abeba in 1960 at a time when the Emperor's son-in-law was Minister of Interior. I knew him quite well, as he had been Governor-General of Begemdir some years before. So I asked him to give me written permission to be allowed to travel throughout Begemdir and preach to all Felashas and K'imants. This was granted and came through in November, so overturning the previous order not to preach outside the two compounds. Had this order been delayed for only one month it would not have reached us, for in December the Commander of the Emperor's Body Guard led a coup d'état while the Emperor was out of the country, which the army quickly overcame. This man had shot a whole room full of the Emperor's closest supporters, but the Minister of Interior escaped with his life by falling down under the other bodies and feigning death.

The main aim of the Families' School was to train men and women to be witnesses back in their villages, not to join the staffs of missions, even our own, and now at last an increasing number of graduates were fulfilling the aim. An extra evangelist was needed to go around to their villages encouraging them, and God provided a man to make use of that permit.

Mengistu Degu was a Felasha Jew with a very chequered history. He had been a servant and soldier to the Italians as a teenager and later went to live near Birra. He obtained a Bible from the Mission in the early days, through which he came to suspect that perhaps Jesus was the Messiah, though not the Son of God. The leader of the Jewish Counter Mission was his relative and persuaded him to go to their school in Asmara for several months. Here he learnt much Hebrew by heart from a Rabbi who did not think it important that he should understand the meaning of it. On returning to his country he taught Felasha children how to read and write Amharic and Hebrew in one of their 35 schools, until lack of funds forced them to close most of these down.

He then tried to enter the Families' Bible School, but was told that it was too obvious why he had come. The Adventists heard of this and welcomed him with open arms, baptised him, and made him a paid evangelist without teaching him. But when he returned to his village his conscience smote him. He refused to take his pay saying that he did not believe the Adventist faith, and then came again to our Bible School. After another two months of testing he was accepted, was eventually truly converted there, and has become one of the evangelists.

All applicants to the Bible School were interviewed on one set day in the year and the choice was made by the majority vote of the evangelists. They favoured men who already knew how to read and write, and who needed therefore to stay two years rather than three to fulfil the course. But invariably their wives were illiterate, so a separate class was created as a finishing class for them. The teacher of this new class was K'es Asris' daughter, Sarah, the first woman graduate, who had gone on to two other Missions and then come back, saying that she had seen much of Addis Abeba and elsewhere, and found no other place where she felt happier about the Bible teaching. This was a steadying influence on some of the young people, many of whom had come to look upon Addis Abeba and some other Missions as their shining goals because of higher pay.

The women were very shy at first and most of them had had little desire to come, but did so only because their husbands made them. Learning texts by heart was the chief thing which led them to Christ, and often this was true of the men too. But it was little meetings, which rose up spontaneously in the compound, which helped most to get them used to spiritual things. The houses of the evangelists were purposely scattered in various parts, and each one drew around him four or five families, sometimes for coffee and prayer, and sometimes for prayer alone, three evenings a week. Many a woman especially would never have learned to pray aloud apart from these little group meetings.

Some missions have based their work on schools for children and have tried to get at the parents through them.

This rarely works. Others have been forced to concentrate on the women for lack of male missionaries. This is not much better. God emphasised whole families in the Bible, and has blessed this emphasis among the Felashas. We did not press for baptism when the first member of a family was converted and ready for it. We waited until the rest of the family was at least willing for baptism and then took the whole family to the priests of the Ethiopian Church. In this way divorce and splits were usually avoided, and many whole families of these Jews have turned to Christ.

We have found that the Spirit of God requires time to enable a Jew to overcome his prejudice against Christianity, and more time to lead him to place his faith in Jesus as his divine Messiah. During the two or three years that the families lived on this compound the needed time could be given, and the Spirit of Christ could work the miracle of turning Jews sincerely to Him.

Shortage of staff

One good result of our continuing shortage of European staff was a concentration on training Ethiopians as Christian leaders, but a bad result was the growing ill health of the three missionaries. We thanked God for the arrival of several nurses and teachers from England, especially after 1963, when we could at last prepare to hand over the Children's Schools to fully trained teachers. Roger and Jean Cowley went on to establish a teachers' training school which produced our own teachers; for some of its graduates were sufficiently conse-crated Christians to resist the great temptation to higher wages elsewhere, in order to teach their own tribe.

Roger went on to start a small Bible School at Jenda for Orthodox priests and deacons, which helped greatly to bring about greater friendship with the Ethiopian Church in the whole area. He felt called of God to concentrate on such work, and a B.C.M.S. missionary helped him with it more than once, bringing students from Addis Abeba to Jenda. Eventually Roger and Jean were seconded to B.C.M.S. and were placed under the direction of the Ethiopian Bishop of Tigrey in 1970, when they started teaching priests and deacons in that province.

Christine and I left for good in 1967, and our place was taken by the Reverend Dr. Ian Lewis, who had arrived in 1966 with his wife and children. They, and the four other missionaries with them, had then only been on the field a short time, and it is a good thing that the Ethiopian evangelists were able to take more responsibility, especially those who were running the Families School on their own.

An indigenous fellowship

Such leaders need to be trained. While Debtera Biru and the four men trained at St. Chrischona were together as a team there was much spiritual fruit, but they did not train any of their converts to succeed them, and so the next generation was disappointing and became spiritually dead.

Our aim was for the Families' Bible School to lead to an indigenous Fellowship of true believers within the Ethiopian Church. But most of the graduates were Felashas, who owned no land and could only rent it from the Amharas. There were no industries in Begemdir and practically no natural resources, and so no trades that the Mission could easily teach them. At the same time they came from villages scattered over such a wide area that the graduates could not easily group together to form such a Fellowship. We tried to start one with a man as leader who would need such further training. He was a converted Felasha who had been a man of violence before he came to the Families' School in 1963. He had fought his own brother in the Courts over certain land rights, and regularly insulted Mengistu Degu whenever he came to his village to witness. Others there had got a name for themselves by murdering men, and he thought seriously of murdering a man who had stolen two bulls from him. But he was impressed by the evangelist's patience and message, and decided that if he were accepted into the Bible School it would perhaps be a sign to him that God did not want him to murder that man!

In the Bible School several texts from Isaiah pointed him away from his false trust in keeping the Saturday Sabbath and other memorial feasts, and pointed him to the Jewish Messiah, the Saviour of the World, Whom he finally started to follow. But neither he nor others have yet reached sufficient depth of spiritual life to make such a Fellowship really viable.

This is not the only man who has confessed to a desire to murder or to live by stealing. It is asking much of any Bible School to raise men from such depths to a height where they can stand firm, and perhaps almost alone, as witnesses for Christ in isolated areas where Ethiopians do not take easily to fellowships of any sort.

Hopes for the future of the Felashas

God seems to be preparing the Jews once again for some key role in the blessing of the world.[j] If so, the Felashas will no doubt have some vital part to play in the blessing of Africa. But their immediate hopes must be bound up with the future of Ethiopia, for they are not a large tribe and very poor. Most of them are trying to plough a few rented fields while being weavers, blacksmiths or pottery makers. All three occupations are gradually becoming redundant. Perhaps an agriculturist missionary could help them most, especially near Mach'a where they have come to own their own land.

At the same time most of them have now decided that their own faith is dying. Their hopes had been set on going to Jerusalem, but the Israelis, and above all the Orthodox Jewish Rabbis there, have rejected them. They were led by monks in a life based on having as little physical contact with people of other faiths as possible. Now the monks have died off, and the advent of modern roads and schools have forced the Felashas out of isolation. But this has also opened up a new way of escape, for the schools are open to all, and they can hide their identity in large towns. This means giving up their own Jewish faith and becoming nominal Amhara Christians, but an increasing number are willing to do this.

However, God has never allowed Jews to be swallowed by the countries of their adoption,[k] and He may well have a better plan for them. But in any case now is the time for Christians everywhere to help them, for never before have they been more open to the claims of Christ. For African Jews to join

(j) Rom. 11. vv. 12, 15, 26. Is. 66 vv. 19-22. Zech 8 vv. 22, 23.
(k) Ezek 20. 32.

an African Church seems fitting, but the Mission wants to make sure that in that process as many as possible shall become real Christians and not just nominal ones.

Dr Ian Lewis has added to our hopes for the future by what has proved to be a wonderful answer to much prayer. He was convinced that he needed to start a third station in Mach'a to the South East of Gonder. Several Felasha families had cleared the bush nearby from about 1950 onwards, and found rich agricultural land for which no Amhara Christian charged rent. Hearing this, hundreds more Jewish families joined them from Lasta and other areas and cleared so much bush that this is now the densest area of Felasha occupation in Ethiopia.

Because I knew well the antiquated system of land tenure by which 50 or 100 relatives can claim the same plot of land, and because I had had enough of court cases, I had made no attempt to rent land which was not in government hands. But Ian was new and went striding ahead in faith after we left. The evangelists worked with him and all persisted even after finding that they needed at least fifty signatures, with six men refusing to sign without a bribe, which was never produced. As they persisted the number of claimants increased, and at each turn and corner the signatures of more government officials were needed too. But in the end they obtained all that were needed—well over 100!

By this time it was the wrong time of year for building. Again they were not deterred, and about three miles of road were built during the rainy season of 1969. Future rains are the less likely to wash this away. Before Ian left for furlough in 1970 the clinic and missionaries' houses and several huts had been built amazingly cheaply. He had left Dabat for Gonder with his family and put up a temporary building just in time to receive, unexpectedly and very cheaply, the surplus building and school material of a Swedish Charitable organisation, which had been building schools in that Province.

As Ian Lewis is a medical doctor, the hope is to teach preventive medicine to the Felashas as widely as possible in that area. This will be greatly helped by a travelling dispensary and other medical supplies which he obtained in 1971 with help from Tear Fund. Such work will be a practical demonstration to the Felashas of the love of God, and a suitable accompaniment to the Gospel.

So two possibilities for the Felashas everywhere are either a devouring, materialistic tragedy, within or without the fold of a nominal Christianity, or the riches of Christ in a revived Ethiopian Church.

Hopes for the future of Ethiopia

Ethiopia has been held together and made great in the past by some great emperors with a loyalty to the Ethiopian Orthodox Church. The advent of modern ideas is now undermining both of these solid foundations. The Emperor Haile Selassie has himself tried to steer the Ethiopians towards parliamentary democracy, but the Amharas especially are never likely to embrace it except as an outward façade.

In this book we have dealt far more with the other foundation to Ethiopian unity, the Church. This has kept the country together many times in the past when loyalty to a legitimate emperor was impossible. But modern ideas are making the people increasingly dissatisfied with services in a dead language and virtually no proper teaching at all. Neither compromise nor time can heal this now, only a radical renewal.

Such renewal came in England largely through the translation of the Bible into the spoken language. More and more Ethiopians are turning to their new translation, and many younger ones are proving that modern education has not turned them away from the basic faith of their fathers. Some of these have started Sunday Schools, women's meetings, broadcasts, and a mission that has begun to reach out to the pagans. B.C.M.S. especially is in happy co-operation with such.

This is a very long step away from the old-fashioned Amhara, who regarded himself as a member of God's chosen race, which has replaced the Jews, for whom to proselytise would be to compromise his own position. Similarly the priests felt that to teach openly mysteries given to them to guard was still more to compromise their privileged position.

Reform of the Church is vital to Ethiopia, and there are

very deep prejudices to be overcome. The alternative is a vacuum which would be extremely dangerous. But we must hope that the African nature of this Church will be preserved wherever possible, while praying Christians everywhere look to God for new life. There are not many Ethiopians as yet who are making this their main aim. Those who do, give great cause for hope for the future of Ethiopia and perhaps of all Africa.

Christianity, even of the Western sort, has proved strong enough already to conquer much of Africa South of the Sahara Desert, but its appeal to the people is limited because it has been interpreted to them by Western missionaries. To give it a deeper meaning for them it must be re-interpreted by Africans. The Coptic Church in Egypt is more Arab than African, and has been for too long subservient to a Moslem government to do much more than survive. The Ethiopian Church, on the other hand, is clearly African and free, yet ancient and non-Western in origin.

Its magnetism for other areas of Africa is demonstrated by the fact that more than one Church or sect, formed by Africans as a protest against Western ways, has called itself by some such name as "The Ethiopian Church." An enlightened secession from that Church could hardly have such an effect, let alone a new denomination started by foreigners.

European music, buildings and art do not appeal to the soul of Africans in the same way as the music, for instance, of the Ethiopian Church, especially when accompanied as it is by drums and the solemn dancing of the Debteras.

Old Testament theology is almost non-existent in most African Churches, yet African thought and life is basically far more akin to the Old Testament than to Greek thought. The Ethiopian Church is based almost as much on the Old Testament as it is on the New, and less on Greek thought than the Western Churches. To interpret the Old Testament to Africans is a part which Felasha converts could play better than anyone else. And the ordination of K'es Asris in 1971 shows that this day may not be so very far off.

The opportunities before the missionaries of the two Societies, C.M.J. and B.C.M.S., in Ethiopia have never been greater, and it is a privilege to support and help them. The potential is tremendous, but the time is short. Therefore "let Ethiopia hasten to stretch out her hands to God". (Psalm 68 verse 31).

BIBLIOGRAPHY

Chapters 1 & 2: Ethiopia and the Felashas

Budge, Sir E. Wallis, "A History of Ethiopia". Methuen & Co. London 1928.

Budge, Sir E. Wallis: "The Queen of Sheba and her only Son Menyelek". Methuen & Co. London. 1932.

Buxton, David: "Travels in Ethiopia". Medill McBride Co. New York. 1949.

Cheeseman, R. E.: "Lake Tana and the Blue Nile". Macmillan. London. 1936.

Faitlovitch, J: "Quer durch Abessinien". Berlin. 1910.

Flad, J. M.: "The Felashas (Jews) of Abyssinia." William Macintosh. London. 1869.

Harris, William C.: "The Highlands of Aethiopia". Longman's. London. 1844.

Hotten, John C.: "Abyssinia and its People". J. C. Hotton. Piccadilly. 1868.

Jager, Otto A.: "Antiquities of North Ethiopia". F. A. Brockhouse. Stuttgart. 1965.

Jones, A. H. M. & Monroe, E.: "History of Abyssinia". O.U.P. London, 1935.

Leslau, Wolf: "Falasha Anthology". Yale University Press. New Haven. 1951.

Levine, Donald N.: "Wax and Gold"—about Ethiopian culture. University of Chicago Press, Chicago and London. 1967.

Mathew, A. F.: (Translator) "The Teaching of the Abyssinian Church". Faith Press. London. 1936.

Moorehead, Alan: "The Blue Nile". Hamish Hamilton. London. 1962.

Mosley, Leonard: "Haile Selassie the Conquering Lion". Wiedenfeld & Nicolson. London. 1964.

Murphey, Dervia: "In Ethiopia with a Mule". John Murray, London. 1968.

O'Hanlon, Douglas: "Features of the Abyssinian Church". S.P.C.K. London. 1946.

Perham, Marjorie: "The Government of Ethiopia". Faber & Faber. London. 1947.

Rathjens, C: "Die Juden in Abessinien". Hamburg. 1921.

Simoons, Frederick J.: "Northwest Ethiopia". University of Wisconsin Press. Madison. 1960.

Stern, H. A.: "Wanderings among the Felashas in Abyssinia". Wertheim, Macintosh & Hunt. London. 1862.

Trimingham, J. Spencer: "Islam in Ethiopia". O.U.P. London. 1952.

Ullendorf, E.: "The Ethiopians: An introduction to country and people". O.U.P. London. 1960.

Universitè de Paris: "Receuil de Textes Felashas". Institut d'Ethnologie Paris. 1951.

Walker, C. H.: "The Abysinnian at Home". The Sheldon Press. London. 1933.

Chapters 3 to 12: The story, etc.

Allen, Roland: "The Spontaneous Expansion of the Church". World-Dominion Press. London. 1956.

Corey, Muriel, W.: "From Rabbi to Bishop". C.M.J. London. 1957.

Flad, C. F. W.: "Abyssinia: A Romance of Missions". CMJ. London.

Flad, Friedrich: "Michael Aregawi". Brunnen-verlag. Basel. 1952.

Flad, J. Martin: "60 Jahre in der Mission unter den Felashas in Abyssinien". Brunnen-verlag. Basel. 1922.

Flad, Pauline: "Ein Braune Perle". Brunnen-verlag. Basel. 1939.

Grubb, Norman: "Alfred Buxton of Abyssinia and Congo". Lutterworth Press. London. 1942.

Isaacs, A. A.: "Biography of H. A. Stern". James Nisbet & Co. London. 1886.

Markham, C. R.: "A History of the Abyssinian Expedition". Macmillan. London. 1869.

Rassam, Horzmud: "Narrative of the British Mission to Theodore, King of Abyssinia. Murray. London. 1869.

Rubenson, Sven: "King of Kings Tewodros of Ethiopia". The University, Addis Ababa. 1966.

(Anonymous) "Samuel Gobat, Bishop of Jerusalem". James Nisbet & Co. London. 1884.

Sandford, Christine: "Ethiopia under Haile Selassie". J. M. Dent. London. 1946.

Walker, T.: "Missionary Ideals". I.V.F. London. 1963.

Published by The Olive Press and printed by
Lawrence-Allen Ltd., Gloucester Street, Weston-super-Mare, Somerset